GREAT SPORTING ECCENTRICS

David Randall

Richardson Steirman & Black

NEW YORK

To my wife Pamela,
in aid of whose accumulated debts
this book had to be written.

Introduction

EVER SINCE *Homo sapiens* first got up on his hind legs, flexed his muscles and found he could kick, throw and push things, he has played games. And when he started playing games he made a second discovery. He found that there was always someone who was not as other sportsmen are.

The oddball was never difficult to spot. When the rest of the tribe went back into the cave after a hard day grunting round the fire, he would be the one who remained outside, refusing to come in until he had hit a dozen pebbles into a hollow tree trunk. Everyone else threw a spear overarm but he would lob it from between his legs; and while other men hunted for food, he hunted for trophies. You could hardly move in his cave for the heads of woolly mammoth mounted on the walls. In other words, Man discovered that when you have sport, you also have sporting eccentrics.

Every age has had them – the Roman chariot fan who was so distraught at his team's defeat that he threw himself on a funeral pyre, the Maharajah who went to war to recover a stolen polo pony, the sixteenth century bowls hooligan, the Restoration lord who went a-leaping, the Georgian duke who proposed to a girl on the strength of her batsmanship, the Victorian lady who knocked out a world heavyweight boxing champion, the Edwardian cricketer who went mad at the crease, the Scotsman who golfed himself to death between the wars and the modern granny who won a weightlifting contest. They are a marvellous breed of lunatics and this book has been written to salute them.

Most are fanatics of one kind or another, diehard enthusiasts who would do anything for their sport – except give it up. They are willing to sweep aside the distractions of poverty, disablement, advancing age, terrorist attacks or wars and get on with something more important, like the 4.30 at Market Rasen or a five foot putt. Theirs is an unswerving devotion, perfectly captured in the pre-1914 rhyme about the player who had been —

'Playing golf when the Germans landed,
And the thought of England's shame
Almost put me off my game.'

Then there are those quirky individuals who have chosen sport as the arena in which to display their weird behaviour. Men like the millionaire cricketer who wore inflatable pads, the baronet who claimed he was the war correspondent for the *Sporting Times*, the singer who played golf in a suit of armour, the cricketer who signed autographs with a rubber stamp and the angler who went fishing in his town's main drainage system. There are also compulsive all-rounders, performers of strange and wonderful feats and, finally, those who have not so much chosen sporting eccentricity but had it thrust upon them.

All the main sports are covered in this book, plus anything from baseball to wrestling and tug-of-war to skydiving. The line, however, had to be drawn somewhere and it has been drawn at some of the more self-consciously freakish activities like golf-cart racing, tobacco-spitting and ice floe sailing. Not, of course, that one doubts the considerable appeal of these pursuits. Indeed, at the US Tobacco Spitting Championships the flower of American manhood standing in a line expectorating at a distant target must be a truly imposing sight. It is simply that in this author's opinion all such activities are not sport.

Acts committed while taking part in sponsored events are similarly banned, on the grounds that the motivation is do-gooding rather than pure sport. But performances while under the influence of a wager are allowed. There is, after all, nothing like the prospect of losing huge sums of money to pep up the contestants. So you will find here not only the Victorian landowner who walked 1,000 miles for a bet but also the man who was so keen to win on the horses that he invented a race meeting, the Oxford undergraduate who dreamt winners and the hardened gambler who even had a flutter on his own death. However, the Cypriot gentleman who asked Corals to quote him odds on his daughter remaining *intacta* while she worked in England as an au pair, is not included. Sadly the young lady was found to be ineligible before coming under starter's orders.

Such exceptions apart, these pages have been open to any legitimate eccentrics — be they players, officials, benefactors, sponsors or fans; fit and with it or lame and loopy. The result is a collection of over 350 specimens aged from five to 104, drawn from 48 sports and 36 countries and covering the years from 536 B.C. to A.D. 1984.

They are as motley a crew as you could ever find. Apart from three Prime Ministers, two American Presidents and an African dictator, there are the creators of Peter Pan and Dracula, a cow, a disgruntled heir to the throne, murderers, drunks, several MPs, a QC, a PC, a VC, the 'It' girl, a weird civil servant, two Kings of England, a dozen vicars, the original real McCoy, a cat, one or two perverts, a notorious gunslinger, an ex-nun, Nell Gwyn's great-grandson, a Nobel prize-winner, two members of the Hell-Fire Club, Lillie Langtry's lover and the England cricket captain who pushed Winston Churchill into the River Thames. These, and all the others in the book, are positive proof that when it comes to inspiring strange behaviour, nothing can match sport.

Author's Note on Sources

ANY BOOK which deals with the amazing and the bizarre is sooner or later liable to prompt the question in the reader's mind, 'Yes, all very amusing and startling, but is it true?' The answer, as far as this volume is concerned, is 'Yes'. But since there will still be those who will not feel inclined to take this general assurance on trust, here are a few words about the sources used or rejected, as the case may be.

There has been something of a trend in publishing recently for books whose material is based on appeals for information. It all sounds so simple. All you have to do is invent a subject, dash off some letters scrounging personal reminiscences and back by return of post comes everything you need to compile *Celebrity Gas Bills* or *Faux Pas of the Famous* or whatever it is.

It might have been tempting to produce this book in the same way: a beguiling letter to sportsmen and sports bodies asking for nominations and, hey presto, before you know where you are, you're all ready for typing. But ever since I read about Sir Theodore Cook I have been wary about appeals for information. Sir Theodore was writing a book on the great racehorse Eclipse and, anxious to leave no avenue unexplored, he appealed for relics of this wonderful beast. Sure enough, in came six complete skeletons, two whole skins and 19 hooves. None of the entries here, you will be pleased to know, are the result of any appeals.

Neither are any of them anonymous. As some writers of books on the curious have discovered, anonymity is a cloak behind which much jiggery-pokery with the facts can be practised. You know the kind of thing – 'An anonymous man who ate 48 pork pies in a minute and then ran backwards up the Empire State Building while playing Handel's 'Messiah' on a ukulele.' It is all very well, but after a few pages the absence of any names begins to nag away at the reader like a bad case of indigestion. For that reason there are no nameless entries in this book.

So, given the self-imposed rule that one must have a few reliable facts to bandy about, where did they come from? A good number of the contemporary items were culled from first-hand accounts and interviews. I work as a sports journalist for the *Observer* which, among other things, has a reputation for having an almost unhealthy interest in the unusual. Thus a large amount of useful information has been fed my way, particularly since we started the Observer Sports Nut of the Year award. Several colleagues, notably Peter Corrigan, Geoffrey Nicholson and Christopher Wordsworth, also put me on the trail of many an interesting character and to them I owe my thanks.

A far larger body of journalists has provided enormous service without knowing it. These are the authors of the many stories of sporting eccentricity that I have been collecting for the last few years. Newspapers, particularly for some reason *The Times* and the *Daily Mail*, produce a regular flow of worthy items. Periodicals are a less fruitful area, although *Sports Illustrated*, *The Cricketer* and *Golf Monthly* are honourable exceptions.

As far as I can discover, there has been no previous publication of a book on sporting eccentrics. This has meant that the books I have consulted are an extraordinarily catholic collection – ranging from a history of costume to a study of the Victorian underworld. This has proved a blessing, for some of the least likely books have contained the choicest tit-bits. For instance, I was aware that K.G. Gandar Dower was a prolific all-rounder in the 1920s but an idle flick through the *Guinness Book of Animal Facts and Feats* revealed that he was also the man behind the most ludicrous experiment in the history of greyhound racing. Equally, a reading of the Revd Francis Kilvert's *Diary*, a volume not normally noted for its sports reporting, threw up the delicious story of the Revd Samuel Ashe and his wholehearted opposition to football. It was not long before one feared to pass over the jottings of even the most obscure clergyman, lest they contain a real prize.

More conventional sports books, both ancient and modern, provided the backbone of many of the historical entries. Some, like *The Encyclopaedia of Sport* edited by Charles Harvey, have given countless leads for further research and a few have even produced stories which are more or less complete in their information. But most books have provided the odd nugget which, when tied up with other material, has enabled me to piece together a total picture. They are all listed in the bibliography, along with every other source.

Of course there are perils with even the most authoritative-looking printed source. A number of cricket books, for example, give the marvellous story of the fanatical captain who was so furious when one of his fieldsmen dropped a catch that he marched over and laid the man out with a right hook to the jaw, the pay-off line being, 'Well, it was a very simple catch.' The only trouble is that I came across the yarn in about half a dozen places and each case involved a different captain in a different match. So this particular authorial finger was raised and the story was dismissed.

Other gems also bit the dust and, in some cases, a new authorised version is given of oft-repeated stories. For example, the Duke of Dorset, several writers tell us, dismissed his mistress from his favours after she ran him out at cricket. Sadly, a slender little volume from the Tate Gallery (*Gainsborough's Giovanna Baccelli* by Elizabeth Einberg) rather wrecks the story by revealing that the mistress referred to was not due in England for another 20 years and anyway the Duke was only nine years of age at the time.

Such experiences made one nervous and the policy has been: if in doubt, leave it out. This, of course, does not guarantee that what remains is the unvarnished and unimpeachable truth, but it does mean that all efforts to make it so have been taken. If any old myths, legends, half-truths and inaccuracies have been unwittingly perpetuated, I would be grateful to have them pointed out for the sake of any possible future editions.

A

Antonio Abertando An Argentinian long distance swimmer who seemed to have no idea when to stop. In the early 1950s, during a marathon swim down the Mississippi River, he lost all sense of feeling and did not realise that leeches had fastened onto his flesh. But it needed more than a few parasites to halt Abertando and despite this grotesque drain on his strength he went on to complete his 262 mile swim in three days 18 hours. He did, however, bear the scars of the experience for the rest of his life.

It should have put him off swimming but it didn't. Even in middle age the man who had twice swum the 168 miles across the River Plate between Argentina and Paraguay, was still setting records. One day in September 1961, for instance, he went for a most extraordinary dip in the sea. Pulling on the white cap which bore the name 'Evita Peron' in honour of his government sponsors, he entered the English Channel off the coast of France. Just 18 hours 50 minutes later he waded ashore near Dover, England. He had five minutes rest on the beach, then strode back into the surf and swam all the way back to France to collect his clothes. The return trip took over 24 hours but the 42-year-old became the first man ever to succeed in a double crossing of the Channel.

William Adlam The world's oldest cricketer. One summer's afternoon at Taunton, Somerset in 1888 he shuffled to the wicket at the ludicrous age of 104. Sadly this one brief innings from the tail-end of his life is all we know of him, the first 103 years of his cricketing career having passed without comment or note.

Anders Ahlgren A Swedish wrestler whose refusal to give way contributed to one of the great stalemates of sport. In the light-heavyweight final at the 1912 Olympics he and Finland's Ivar Bohling struggled and strained for over nine hours without either of them gaining a fall. The Games officials, appalled at the thought of a re-match, awarded them both silver medals. Ever since this bout Greco-Roman wrestling has had trouble in establishing itself as a major spectator sport.

Dr Israr Ahmed Pakistani theologian and spoilsport. In 1982 he persuaded his government to stop men from watching women's sports events. He was afraid that male bystanders would be inflamed by a glimpse of sporting thigh. A year later the good doctor's study of the infinite and ultimate bore further fruit when he publicly declared cricket to be 'a game of eunuchs which wastes the nation's precious time'. Outraged to be thus no-balled, a Punjabi lawyer then sued him for gross defamation of the game and its followers.

Marquis of Ailesbury (1861–1894) A racing man and general ne'er do well. He was so fond of gambling, but so poor a judge of horseflesh, that by the age of 28 he had run up debts of £345,462. Not that it was easy – indeed he only succeeded by behaving like a madman at every available opportunity – but he did have the advantage of starting young. He left Eton under something of a cloud, having refused to be birched for impertinence to the headmaster, and before he was even out of his teens had taken to the Turf and begun his systematic and profligate disposal of the family fortune.

For reasons best known to himself, he aped the manners and dress of what his relatives would no doubt have called the 'riff-raff'. He wore a cabman's heavy box coat with half-crowns instead of buttons, shunned his social equals and fraternised with jockeys and tipsters. Soon he was speaking like them too, becoming fluent in Cockney rhyming slang and answering to the name of 'Billy Stomachache' (which was easier on the proletarian tongue than his real moniker of George William Thomas Brudenell-Bruce). He completed the act by marrying an actress called Dolly Tester, who sounds as if she might have been fun but rather expensive. She left him after 18 months.

All the while his racing losses were mounting. When his liquid assets finally ran dry he began to work his way through the family estates in Wiltshire and Yorkshire. But it was soon obvious that he would require an acreage the size of the Russian Steppes to fund his debts. More desperate measures were called for and, using his position as an owner, he began fixing races. Billy was not, however, the most discreet of men and he was soon rumbled. At the York meeting in August 1887 he ordered the jockey to 'pull' his horse Everitt in the Harewood Stakes. The stewards cottoned on, reported him and he was expelled from the Jockey Club for fraud.

He spent the last years of his brief but costly life in a suburban villa in Brixton subsisting on £20 a week. The deprivations of scraping by on only about ten times the average wage were almost more than Billy could stand. Shortly before his death he said, 'It's hard times. In the old days I used to give the dog a roast fowl. Now I can hardly afford a bird myself.'

Arnold Alcock The man who played for England by mistake. He was a very ordinary rugby union player for Guy's Hospital and so he was completely dumbfounded when he received a letter inviting him to play for his country against South Africa in 1906. Mind you, the England secretary was equally amazed on the day of the match to see Alcock lug his bag into the Crystal Palace dressing room and report for international duty.

After a brief and initially bewildering conversation all became clear. The coveted letter calling Alcock to the England colours should in fact have been sent to one Andrew Slocock of Liverpool. Obviously at this late stage it was impossible to change the team and so Alcock played. There was, however, to be no storybook ending. The match was a less than thrilling 3-3 draw and the unexpected debutante duly returned to the obscurity of his hospital side. Later that season justice was done; Slocock played for England against France and went on to earn seven more caps.

Robert Barclay Allardice (1779–1854) A Scottish landowner with an insatiable appetite for running and walking. For ten years at the beginning of the nineteenth century he was the fastest thing on two legs. As a result he became the first man to make a fortune at athletics.

Allardice succeeded to his father's estates in Scotland when he was 18 and within a few years was regularly wagering large amounts of his inheritance on his ability to tramp vast distances. In 1800 he bet 1,000 guineas that he could walk 90 miles in 21½ hours but caught a cold and lost. He upped the ante to 2,000 guineas but lost again. By 1801 the stake had reached 5,000 guineas and this time, on November 10, he succeeded with over an hour to spare, covering the distance in 20 hours 22 minutes and 4 seconds.

For eight years Allardice, popularly known as Captain Barclay, had no match at running or walking. Some put his pre-eminence down to his diet: lean beef or mutton, butter, cheese and strong ale, but never any milk. Others ascribed it to his training regime: purging and sweating by walking swathed in clothes and lying between feather mattresses. But the secret was really his own outlandish talent, allied to a lifestyle in which a 30 mile walk was commonplace.

In 1808, for example, he spent three days in this fashion – starting at 5 a.m. he walked 30 miles while on a grouse shoot, dined, walked 60 miles back to his house in 11 hours, attended to business, walked 16 miles to Laurence Kirk, danced at a ball, returned home by 7 a.m. and spent that day partridge shooting. Just to fulfill the normal round of social and business engagements he had covered 130 miles on foot and gone without sleep for two nights.

With this kind of preparation he was ready in 1809 for his greatest feat: 1,000 miles in 1,000 hours. Setting off across Newmarket Heath on 1 June, he averaged a mile every 14 minutes and 54 seconds in the first week and managed to maintain a pace only marginally slower until, on 12 July, he finished in triumph. He had lost over two stone in weight but won £16,000 in wagers. Five days later he embarked with the 23rd Regiment for the Walcheren Campaign.

When he returned from the wars he gave no more public performances. Allardice devoted himself to improving the local breeds of cattle and pressing his claims to the earldoms of Airth, Strathern and Monteith. He never succeeded, surely the greatest athlete never to win a title.

E.B. Alletson The source of the most baffling cricket mystery of all time. One May day in 1911 Alletson of Nottinghamshire left the Hove pavilion and arrived at the crease a tail-ender of unmitigated incompetence. He departed it, an hour and a half of playing time later, as the scorer of the most outrageous innings in the history of county cricket. In a frenzy of wild hitting he made 189 runs in just 90 minutes.

Going in at number 11 he scored a relatively subdued 47 in the 50 minutes before lunch. But he emerged from the interval like a man possessed and between 2.15 and 2.55 savaged the Sussex attack. In these 40 minutes he hit 142 runs, striking with such ferocity that one ball was embedded in the soft timbers of the pavilion and several fieldsmen were injured. Some bowlers were said to have never recovered from the mauling, poor Killick in particular whose two overs cost 56 runs. Whatever madness descended on the Nottingham man, it never visited him again and eventually Alletson was dropped from the side.

H.H. Almond A nineteenth century schoolmaster whose headship of Loretto School was distinguished by an obsession with games so maniacal that it injured his health. His excitement when watching even a junior house football match reached such a violent pitch that in later life he had to be restrained by force from spectating, lest a seizure overwhelm him.

V. Ambramov A Russian footballer and the patron saint of all professional sportsmen who are dogged off the field by loudmouths. After a game for Topolsk Dinamo in 1983 he was accosted in a restaurant by a man who, like many sports spectators down the ages, assumed that along with his ticket he had purchased the right to shout offensive and ill-informed abuse at players wherever he found them.

At first Ambramov thought that the fellow's wild gesticulations and inhuman noises were some sort of critique of his side's general strategy. But then he realised that they were in fact a somewhat intimate reference to his own performance. So he took the fan outside and stabbed him. Ambramov was jailed for ten years and his side lost a valued supporter.

Idi Amin The single most persuasive piece of evidence that boxing causes brain damage. In 1951 he won the heavyweight championship of Uganda and defended it for nine years. Later in life he took power in that country and threw his weight around in a far more sinister fashion. He never forgot boxing, however, and one of his few harmless acts as dictator was to declare himself heavyweight champion of the nation for life.

'Foot' Anakin A publican whose skill with a set of darts in the tense atmosphere of a Yorkshire courtroom ensured that the game could be played and enjoyed by future generations.

In 1908 he was prosecuted for allowing darts, then regarded as a game of chance, on his licensed premises. When the case began the prosecution lawyers entered Leeds Magistrates' Court under the weight of sheaves of beribboned documents. Anakin, however, walked in carrying only his arrows and a dartboard. After the learned submissions had been made, the landlord set up his board, withdrew the requisite four paces and showed that darts could not possibly be a game of chance by firing all three projectiles into the single 20.

The bench, warming to the idea of trial by darts, then asked the junior clerk of the court to have a go at hitting the 20. His first two darts missed the board completely; only the final one stuck in and that was a long way from the target. Anakin then took the darts and threw three double 20s. His accuracy was making large holes in the prosecution's case and these widened considerably when he nonchalantly repeated the double top performance. The magistrates, duly impressed, dismissed the case and darts in pubs became legal.

Fred Archer (1857–1886) Probably the greatest and certainly the most dedicated jockey of all time. At 5 foot 9 inches tall and with a winter weight of 11

IDI AMIN

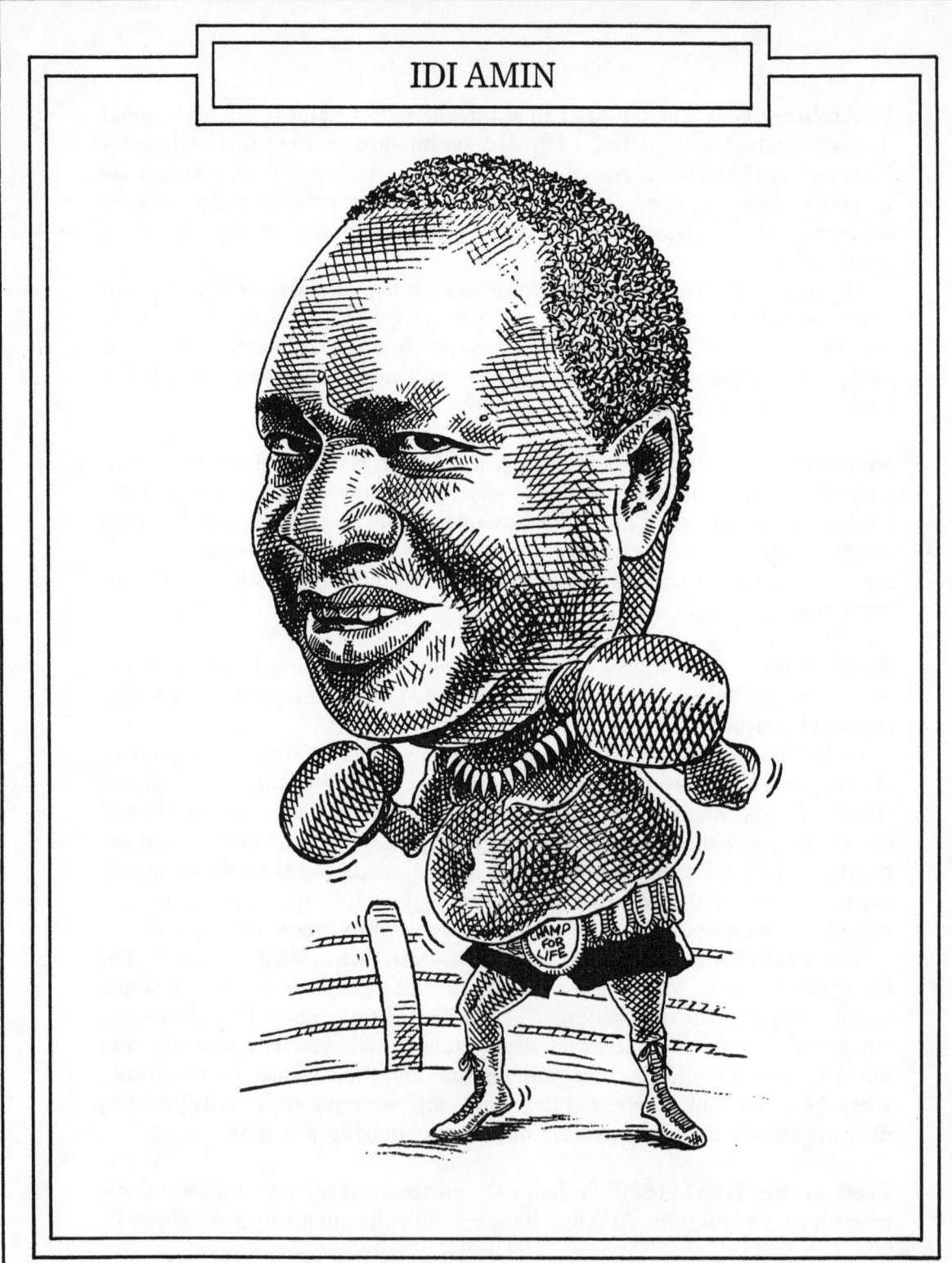

Ugandan heavyweight champion and despot

stone, Archer was entirely the wrong build for a jockey. Yet by subjecting himself to the most appalling deprivations he made his riding weights and rode 2,748 winners.

His diet was so strict that for all his adult life he lived on not much more than the scent of victory. By the age of 18 his daily intake was hot castor oil and half an orange for breakfast and a sardine and a little champagne for dinner. If even this failed to suppress his weight, he would resort to his 'special mixture' – a purgative prepared by Dr Wright, his Newmarket doctor. The concoction was so potent that when a friend tried it he was ill for a week. Archer also spent hours on end sweating in steam rooms.

This regime made him champion jockey at 16 and his fierce urge to win made sure that he kept the title for every one of the remaining 13 years of his life. He won five Derbys, six St Legers, four Oaks, four Two Thousand Guineas and two One Thousand Guineas. Even off the course he could hardly be ignored: he dressed like a curate, had the demeanour of an undertaker and, like many successful men, had an aversion to carrying cash and rarely did so.

In 1884, after his wife of less than two years died in childbirth, he became even more fanatical about his racing. For the next two seasons he rode and dieted like a mad thing. Lord Allington warned him, 'No man can live on two oysters, one prawn, three doses of physic and three Turkish baths daily.' He was right and in the autumn of 1886 the reckoning came. One Monday morning, with his constitution sapped by constant wasting, his body racked by convulsions and his spirits depressed by a losing run, Archer called for his sister. He then took the silver plated pistol he had been given after winning the Liverpool Cup on Sterling and shot himself in front of her. He was 29.

William Archer The story of this jump jockey and the older brother of Fred is a terrible warning to all those tempted to heed the sporting advice given by old men.

One day in 1878 William returned from the races and witnessed a coaching accident outside his parents' hotel. Being a superstitious fellow he believed this to be a portent of his own death if he raced the following day. He decided to cancel his rides. But his father, a practical old buffer, poo-poohed his son's talk of omens and urged him to ride. William was reminded that in his own day his father was good enough to win the Grand National and so he relented. Against all his own better instincts he reported for duty.

Sure enough in a £5 selling hurdle against two other mounts, William suffered a hideous fall and in due course died from his injuries. He had listened to the voice of experience for the last time.

Argonauts A team of football-mad amateurs who had such severe delusions of grandeur that just a few months after their formation in 1928 they applied for membership of the Football League. The following year they tried again and failed. So in 1930, suspecting that their sincerity was in doubt, they coupled their application to the Third Division (South) with a provisional booking of Wembley Stadium as their home ground. League clubs were appalled at their effrontery and the Argonauts polled no votes.

Valerio Arri An Italian long distance runner whose joy at winning the bronze medal in the 1920 Olympic marathon in Antwerp was so unconfined that he managed to find the energy to perform cart-wheels as he crossed the finishing line.

Revd Samuel Ashe The eccentric nineteenth century rector of Langley Burrell in Wiltshire and a good-humoured opponent of sport on the Sabbath. His guerilla war against local footballers was conducted on Langley Common. He would sneak up there and conceal himself under the trees, biding his time until the football came in his direction. When it did this lively old cleric would dart out, robes flowing, and capture the ball. With a strangled cry of triumph he would then pierce the bladder with a pin.

After the first performance of this curious ritual, the players took the precaution of carrying a spare. And so on Sunday after Sunday the Revd Ashe would puncture the ball, only to see a reserve produced, inflated and put into play. At this he would exclaim, 'Ah well, I suppose it must go on,' and disappear muttering back towards his church.

A.J. Atfield On the June morning in 1903 that this Gloucestershire cricketer married he was content in the knowledge that he would be spending the rest of the day with the love of his life. For, shortly after the ceremony at St George's, Hanover Square, the romantic young soul left his bride of a few moments, hurried off to Lord's and scored a century before lunch in the Cross Arrows match. So far as is known, the groom, who wore white on his wedding day, played happily ever after.

Fahmy Attallah The man who spent well over a day unsuccessfully trying to swim across the English Channel – and still would not give up. He was a middle-aged official at the Egyptian Ministry of Commerce and his dogged performance came in the 1950 *Daily Mail* Cross-Channel Race. Swimming old-fashioned breaststroke, he left France at 3 a.m. on 22 August and made his painstaking way towards England. By the time he was in sight of the White Cliffs of Dover, the reception committee on the beach had long since dismantled their tents and most of his fellow competitors were tucked up in bed. Attallah, however, was determined to finish, even if it took all night.

He might have succeeded by then, had it not been for one or two little diversions. First there was a violent thunderstorm, followed by a bout of the cramps. Then the army started firing six inch shells into what it thought was an unoccupied sea. Finally he had an attack of delirium which so affected his sense of direction that he actually swam backwards for a while. These, however, were minor inconveniences; what really scuppered his chances were the tides. Twice he got to within a few hundred yards of the shore and twice he was forced back. He even tried waiting for the tide to turn by resting on his back with his legs tucked up under his chin. But it was hopeless, as everyone out in the Channel could see. Everyone, that is, except Attallah himself.

As his swim entered its second day the organisers gave up pleading with him to retire and, fearing he would soon be drowned, they disqualified him. Twice Attallah and his trainer ignored the officials and finally the accompanying boatman leant out and laid an illegitimate but merciful hand on the Egyptian. It was all over. He had been in the water for 27½ hours, longer than any other Channel swimmer in history and nearly 17 hours more than the winner. It was his sixth Channel failure but his spirit was unbroken. As his comatose little body was borne in the launch towards the shore and hospital, he suddenly sat bolt upright, called weakly, 'I could have done it, you know' and fell back into the arms of his trainer.

Mr Georgius Averoff A wealthy Greek businessman and Olympic benefactor. He was so keen to see a home victory in the marathon at the 1896 Athens Games that he offered the hand of his daughter in marriage to any of his countrymen who might win. Fortunately for the demure Miss Averoff, the Greek winner Spiridon Louis was already married with two children and was quite content with a laurel wreath and the gift of a watercart for his village.

Perhaps it was just as well, for the Olympics had cost the generous Mr Averoff enough already. When plans to revive the ancient games looked doomed it was he who came forward with his ample funds and undertook to pay for the reconstruction of the Olympic stadium. The bill came to 920,000 drachmas.

Abdul Aziz An unfortunate Pakistani cricketer, immortalised in the scorebook for the Quaid-I-Azam Trophy final in Karachi in 1959. His entry reads:

First Innings
Abdul Aziz retired hurt 0

Second Innings
Abdul Aziz did not bat, dead 0

B

Mike Bagley When he was booked for bad language during a game in December 1983 this Bristol footballer was so annoyed that he seized the referee's notebook and ate it. But his attempt to destroy the evidence failed. His league banned him for six weeks.

Harry Bagshaw Even the most ardent sports nut is prepared to concede that death puts a fairly sizable obstacle between him and the game he loves. Bagshaw, however, was an exception. This Derbyshire bowler and umpire saw no earthly reason why his demise should separate him from his cricket. So when his mortal innings closed in 1927 old Harry was interred in Eyam churchyard dressed in his umpire's coat and clutching a cricket ball in his lifeless hand. Above the now horizontal official was set a most impressive tombstone depicting an umpire's hand with index finger raised, signalling 'Out'. Beneath was carved a set of broken stumps with dislodged bails.

Fred Baldesare In July 1962 this American swimmer made the first invisible crossing of the English Channel. Witnesses saw him enter the sea off Cap Gris Nez in France and emerge onto the beach at Sandwich in Kent 18 hours 1 minute later; but no one saw him in between. The reason was that Baldesare swam the whole distance of 42 miles underwater. With the aid of an aqualung he had become the first man ever to do so.

Kenneth Henry Highett Baily (b. 1911) Bournemouth civil servant who decided in the mid-1960's that he would become Britain's sporting mascot. So he ordered a John Bull outfit, equipped himself with a flag and began attending every major international fixture that he could. Since then he has not missed a single England soccer match and has supported his country at many other events including rugby internationals, Davis Cup tennis matches and Olympic Games.

His uniform consists of a top hat, red hunting coat, Union Jack waistcoat, white trousers and a dotty smile. His big moment at each occasion comes when he parades the flag around the stadium before the start or at half-time. For his trouble he is rewarded with a fair share of abuse, and not just from irate foreigners. Once, when Prince Charles was introduced to the fancy-dressed Baily, he took one look at him and asked, 'Where did you escape from?'

Undeterred by this, or some of the less friendly insults he receives, the fanatical old age pensioner continues to support British teams wherever they are competing. He travels all over the world and in 1982 estimated that he had spent over £10,000 on his patriotic hobby. Some years ago, in recognition of Baily's services to Britain, sport and strange behaviour, he was awarded his nation's highest accolade: he had a pub named after him. A likeness of this wonderful and slightly deranged-looking figure now adorns 'The Sportsman' in Pennington, Hampshire.

George Alexander Baird (1857–1893) Sportsman he may have been, but this millionaire went about his fun and games in such a disgraceful way that he became one of the most notorious men in late Victorian England. On the Turf he was an unscrupulous owner, inveterate gambler and by common consent the dirtiest rider alive, while around the boxing ring his misbehaviour was so gross that it made him an outcast, even in the semi-criminal circles he inhabited. Then there was his appetite for the very lowest of blood sports. He maintained and bet heavily on a flock of gamecocks and once, in one of his more inspired moments, he turned the foyer of the Haymarket Theatre into a rat pit.

What one might call his private life, had it not been conducted in a blaze of notoriety, was equally adventurous. He was expelled from Eton not once but twice, was sent down from university, seduced the Marquess of Ailesbury and then eloped with her and was Lillie Langtry's lover until he beat her up once too often. These activities, however, were no more than hobbies. Sport was his consuming interest and provided his life's twin ambitions: to have the winner in at least one major horse race somewhere on earth everyday and to develop a heavyweight boxer who would capture the heavyweight title from John L. Sullivan.

Drawing on his huge income from coalmines – it was said to be £¼ million even when he was at Cambridge – Baird pursued both these aims to the hilt. Not content with one racing stable, he had two. One was at Lickfield where he kept over 100 horses in training and the other was at Moulton Paddocks, Newmarket, which was home for 150 thoroughbreds. From out of these connections came both Oaks and Derby winners and enough good horses in 1887 to make him the leading owner. But it was never sufficient for him to achieve his goal.

He frequently rode his own horses and used, as he did for all his racing enterprises, the *nom de course* of 'Mr Abingdon'. His determination to win verged on the maniacal. In the struggle to keep his weight down he subsisted for long periods on little more than weak tea, castor oil and neat brandy, but once he was in shape he thought little of chartering a special train in order to ride at some-out-of-the-way meeting. When he got there he was liable to use tactics more associated with the Coliseum in Rome than the English Turf. The result was often disqualification, as at Wolverhampton when he tried to barge Lord Hartington and the favourite through the rails.

His gambling was prodigious and sometimes paid off in the most unexpected of ways. It brought him, for example, his most glamorous conquest, for he introduced himself to Lillie Langtry by presenting her with two betting slips, worth £100 the pair. The money was spent on a roistering night out and they became lovers, albeit of the most tempestuous kind. She had much to put up with. Once she was resting at home when an excitable messenger dashed in with the news that there was a riot going on at the Haymarket Theatre, where she was then appearing. She arrived there to find that Baird and some chums had turned the foyer into a rat pit. In an impromptu ring, terrier dogs and great black rats were thrashing about in tooth and claw combat as a frenzied throng – with Baird at their head – shouted the odds and wagered on the bloody outcome. Lillie turned on her heels and was off.

Nevertheless she tolerated this and all the rough stuff he handed out until, in 1892, he hit her so hard that she landed in hospital. She was not, of course, the first woman he had used as a punchbag and one had even sued him. But his taste was really for more equal opposition and he frequently scoured the East End streets looking for a chance to use his ready fists. Boxing was always an obsession with him and in order to try and fulfill his second great ambition he founded a stable of fighters under the management of Charlie Mitchell, an old boxer and Baird's lifelong companion and minder. None of his protégés, however, turned out to be much more than a competent brawler.

Boxing also brought him into the Pelican Club – a shady forerunner of the National Sporting Club – which had aristocratic links despite being founded by two charmers named 'The Shifter' and 'Swears' Wells. For several years Baird was in the thick of the Pelican's ring activities. Until, that is, he excelled himself at an illicit barefist fight that the club had arranged in Bruges. Accompanied by some uglies, he had gone over for the bout anxious to see the object of his vast bet, Jem Smith, defeat his Australian opponent. However, by the 15th round Smith had taken such a hiding that it was obvious he could not last much longer.

Baird had seen enough. Awash with alcohol, he rose up from the crowd and urged his supporters to 'do in the Australian bastard'. All hell broke loose and only the courage of Lord Mandeville, who drew a bowie knife and forced the mob to retreat, prevented a blood bath. As a result of this unedifying episode Baird was thrown out of the Pelican. He tried to have his expulsion ruled illegal by the Chancery Court but failed and so, early in 1893, he went to America. The purpose of the trip was to match his man Mitchell against world heavyweight champion Jim Corbett. While in New Orleans he seconded for Jem Hall against Bob Fitzsimmons, went on a 72-hour drinking binge afterwards and caught pneumonia. He was taken back to his hotel room and there, in the arms of the faithful Mitchell, he died aged 36.

Arthur Balfour A sensible statesman who thought that winning a golf club competition was more important than becoming Prime Minister. In the early years of the century, as the great issues of Free Trade, war with the Boers, the Balkan question and re-armament swirled about him, he wrote to Lady Desborough, 'I have done nothing important or distinguished since we met except to win the handicap prize, value £4–10/- at North Berwick. This has caused far more emotion and surprise in my family than did my becoming Prime Minister. Doubtless it is also more important.'

Perhaps the greatest service he performed for mankind was the favour he did his friend Major Walter Clopton Wingfield. The major had invented a game called Sphairistike which had taken the nation's country houses by storm. It was Balfour who suggested the more catchy name of 'Lawn Tennis' and we must all be grateful that he did.

Mr Baker After a lifetime of dodging His Majesty's customs officers this former smuggler put the exercise to good use as a pedestrian of noted and unusual durability. He specialised in walking round and round in circles for days on end – a puzzling occupation even for the early nineteenth century. His pioneering work was first demonstrated in 1816 when he continuously lapped a common near Rochester for 21 days. By the time he came to a halt he had covered a distance of 1,010 miles. A year later he re-doubled his efforts and strode round Wormwood Scrubs for 42 days to complete a total of 2,000 miles.

Sidney George Barnes An Australian cricketer who never let slip an opportunity to show his contempt for authority. While other players were showing officialdom a degree of deference that would ill-become even a galley slave, Barnes was the master of every species of insolence, from the dumb to the resoundingly vocal.

His good-humoured insubordination first surfaced during a tour match in England in 1948. An appeal, delivered with the strenuous indignation that only Australians can manage, was turned down by umpire Skelding. Just then a dog ran onto the field. Barnes, certain that only an imperfection of sight could have caused the umpire to deny the appeal, gathered the animal in his arms and carried it to Skelding. As he dropped it at the umpire's feet he remarked, 'You've got the dog, now all you need is a white stick.'

Four years later, while serving as captain of New South Wales, he was again outraged by the spurning of an appeal which he thought quite legitimate. This time he took sterner steps – towards the pavilion in fact, with his loyal teammates trailing in his angry wake. The umpires ordered their return and Barnes, to their surprise, complied. But the last word, as usual, was with him. As soon as his side was assembled in the middle, he ordered drinks, even though there was less than 20 minutes to go before tea.

With three Test centuries to his credit, he was good enough for the selectors to forgive him all but his worst excesses. Dark mystery still surrounds most of these misdemeanours, for the usual procedure, as when he was dropped for the Third Test against the West Indies in 1952, was for the Australian Board of Control to simply issue a bald communiqué saying that Barnes had been omitted 'on grounds other than cricketing ability'.

But whether in the side or out, third man or twelfth man, he was always able to find some way to make his bolshie point. Perhaps his finest hour was in 1953 when, having been passed over for the Test against South Africa, Barnes asked to be twelfth man for New South Wales at Adelaide. The unsuspecting state authorities agreed. When the time came for the drinks interval Barnes made his inimical appearance. In the company of the bar steward, he strode to the square attired in a grey suit adorned with a red carnation. He carried a tray on which was placed a scent spray, portable radio and cigars which he then proceeded to offer with due ceremony to players and umpires alike.

This delightful man, who avenged himself on troublesome autograph hunters by signing their books with a rubber stamp, died in 1973.

J.M. Barrie (1860–1937) The diminutive author of *Peter Pan*. At Dumfries Academy he developed a passion for cricket which sustained him through a life unusually beset by tragedy. A brother was killed in a skating accident, his mother and a sister died prematurely, another sister's fiancé received fatal injuries falling from a horse that Barrie had given the couple, two of his adopted sons died tragically early deaths and his wife, upon whom he intermittently doted, conducted an affair which led to their divorce. But through all these losses, his cricket, a game that he called 'an idea of the Gods', remained with him.

At the age of 27 and already a successful author, he founded his own side which he called the 'Allahakbarries'. This curious name was derived from 'Allah akbar', the Arabic for 'heaven help us' – which was no doubt thought riotously funny at the time but must have worn rather thin at the umpteenth request for an explanation. Barrie led this rum collection of friends and fellow authors like P.G. Wodehouse against teams of pressman, actors and villages. Their fixtures with the artists were often styled 'Test' matches.

The tiny enthusiast was barely five foot high and when equipped for the crease looked as if he was trying to conceal himself behind a pair of pads. With his pipe in his mouth he would stride to the wicket, determined always to abide by the motto he had set for his team, 'Should you hit the ball, run at once. Don't stop to cheer.' He once said of his batting in an important match that he scored one run in the first innings but 'in the second I was not quite as successful.'

His bowling he apparently divided into two categories. The good, he said, was so slow that after each delivery he would sit on the turf at mid-off and wait for the ball to reach the other end 'which it sometimes did'. The bad, he regretted, was even slower, so that if he was displeased with a delivery he would be able to run after the ball and bring it back. Sir Arthur Conan Doyle, who was a frequent cricket companion, believed much of this talk to be unduly false modesty. 'Barrie was no novice,' he maintained, 'he bowled an insidious left-hand good length ball coming in from leg which was always likely to get a wicket.'

The Allahakbarries were finally disbanded in 1913, as was Barrie himself some 24 years later.

S.R. Bastard The most appropriately named referee in the history of association football. Hailing from Upton Park, London, he officiated over the FA Cup Final between the Wanderers and Royal Engineers in 1878.

Rudolph Bauer Every athlete dreams that one day he will stand to honoured attention on top of the Olympic victory rostrum. With a medal round his neck, a lump in his throat and a tear in his eye, he will watch his country's flag unfurl to the tune of his national anthem.

That fantasy was about to be fulfilled for Rudolph Bauer from Hungary when he climbed the dais after winning the discus at the 1900 Games in Paris. All, however, was not as it should be. Bauer was not a sentimental man but he had rather set his heart on both flag and music being distinctly Hungarian. Imagine, therefore, his surprise when the American star-spangled banner began cranking up the mast to the strains of 'Hail to the Chief'.

Bauer leapt from the rostrum in a patriotic fury and, after a violent argument with the French officials, he refused to resume his place until a Hungarian flag was found. One was located and on being reassured that the correct sheet music had been distributed to the band, Bauer stepped once more onto the victor's podium. Sure enough, as the Hungarian colours jerked up the pole, the band launched into – the Austrian national anthem. Bauer left Paris at once.

Irving Baxter (1876–1957) The American and Olympic pole vault champion, he arrived at the 1901 Amateur Athletic Association Championships without his pole, something of a disadvantage in that event. His fellow competitors saw a chance to defeat their talented rival and refused to lend him theirs. This so angered Baxter that he uprooted a nearby flagpole, used that and shared the title at 9 foot 10 inches.

Richard Baxter A seventeenth century bore and Puritan whose chief pleasure in life was to stop other people from having any. In his handbook for spoilsports *A Christian Directory*, published in 1678, he may well have stumbled upon the clinical cause of sporting eccentricity. He wrote, 'Watch against inordinate sensual delight in even the lawfullest of sports. Excess of pleasure in any such vanity doth very much corrupt and befool the mind.' So now we know.

Lord Frederick Beauclerc D.D. (1773–1850) Vicar of St Albans, great grandson of King Charles II and Nell Gwyn and a devious early cricketer. This 'amateur' once openly admitted that his match-making at the game brought him in 600 guineas a year. But the means by which he earnt this sum would have shamed a Mississippi steamboat gambler, let alone a man of the cloth. Lord Frederick would often bribe Bentley, the official scorer, and he was not above feigning disablement to hoodwink the opposition.

When appearing at a ground where he was not generally known he would lurch to the wicket with his left shoulder carried higher than his right in imitation of some distressing handicap. He would often increase his apparent deformity by stuffing pocket handkerchiefs under his cricketing waistcoat. But one day he rather overdid the padding and a contemporary said that when Beauclerc returned to the pavilion he reminded him of 'crooked back Richard' – a reference to England's most disfigured monarch.

The odd thing was that there was no particular need for these deceits. He was, in fact, a batsman of high class and would sometimes demonstrate his contempt for the bowler by hanging a valuable gold watch from his middle stump and defying them to hit it. He was president of the MCC in 1826 but retired from the game in a huff when he found that overarm bowling was being tolerated. The Turf was his other passion and the crafty old doctor of divinity would ride and race horses under a pseudonym to avoid the wrath of his bishop. In his later years he managed to happily combine his secular and sacred devotions by having the pulpit at his church in St Albans fitted with a saddle from which he would preach.

Max Beerbohm (1872–1956) Noted Edwardian writer and anti-sport agitator of some wit. Writing in the *Daily Mail* in 1897, he proposed that Queen Victoria's Diamond Jubilee be commemorated by the abolition of the Boat Race. Rowing was not his only aversion. When he was solicited on behalf of the testimonial fund for W.G. Grace, he subscribed a shilling, 'not in support of cricket but as an earnest protest against golf.'

Sir Frank Benson (1858–1939) Oxford athletics blue who went on to become a great actor-manager and an even better cricket nut. He always believed that an actor's usefulness was enhanced by sporting prowess and he once placed an advertisement in a theatrical paper which read, 'Wanted: an actor to play Laertes and Lysander, preferably a slow left arm bowler. Apply Benson Company.'

Bessie A cow and cricket spectator of long standing. The field that she occupied adjoined the premises of the Pentenstall Cricket Club in Bedfordshire and the many summers that she spent grazing there must have caused her to wonder what a cricket ball tasted like. So when one day in 1955, during a pre-match warm-up, a batsman hit the ball into her meadow, she ate it. Sadly it was the club's only one and the game had to be abandoned.

Mr Alfred Bloomingdale The owner of the famous New York department store and a sporting benefactor or rare ingenuity. When he discovered some months before the 1908 Olympics that one of the clerks in his employ was a promising marathon runner, he ordered the construction of a cinder track on the roof of his store so that the athlete could train during his breaks.

The roof-top runner was called John Hayes and when he was eventually selected for the American team, Bloomingdale gave him full holiday with pay to go to the London Games. Hayes duly won the gold medal and his employer, perhaps with half an eye on the publicity value, made him manager of the sporting goods department.

John Mary Pius Boland (1870–1955) An Irishman of intense modesty, he was persuaded to enter the 1896 Olympic tennis tournament while on a touring holiday of Greece. He then proceeded casually to win both the singles and the doubles titles. Boland later became a barrister, MP for South Kerry and Parliamentary Whip for the Irish Nationalist Party. But he was so self-effacing that never in any interview did he ever refer to his gold medals. His only known vanity concerned his curious middle names. Such was his dislike of them that he used to fine each of his relatives sixpence every time they failed to call him John. As befits an Irish patriot he died on St Patrick's Day.

David Bonn In 1982 this son of the Cayman Isles manager gave what is arguably the most bizarre performance in the history of the Commonwealth Games. Bonn was entered for the 10,000 metres in Brisbane and, long before the finish, officials had begun to suspect that his preparation must have lacked a certain thoroughness. Maybe it was the fact that he had to borrow a pair of shorts before the start or his tell-tale sloth in the first hundred metres. It may even have been the way in which all his 16 rivals had passed him twice before they had run seven laps.

But whatever it was, by the eighth circuit, when the leader lapped him for the second time, it was certain that Bonn would not be featuring among the medallists. Indeed, when they broke the tape, he still had seven laps to go. The timekeeper, who might just as well have used a sundial rather than a watch for Bonn, finally clocked him in at 41 minutes 21 seconds.

Glenn Bonnell When this football fan was asked to choose between his wife and the team he supported, he unhesitatingly plumped for the latter. He lived in Penwortham, Lancashire and idolised Celtic, a side who play 189 miles away in Glasgow. This involved him in travelling thousands of miles and spending hundreds of pounds every soccer season. Not surprisingly his wife felt that his money and time could be used to better effect and in 1984, after 11 years as a football widow, she gave him an ultimatum, 'It's either me or the team.'

Bonnell chose Celtic and went to live in digs while his wife returned to her mother. He said, 'I can't really blame Carole. She never understood my passion for Celtic and we had a lot of rows because I was always away. Following the lads takes nearly all my money and my mates say I'm crazy. But I don't care. I just can't give it up.'

John Boot Cricket's most deadly runner between the wickets. Going for a dodgy single and no doubt a little rusty at the beginning of the season, Boot collided with his batting partner during a match in Newark, Nottinghamshire and died from his injuries. He was laid to rest on 14 May 1737.

Horatio Bottomley (1860–1933) A rogue businessman and tub-thumping politician, he had the bright idea of using his racehorses to help get himself elected to Parliament. He was standing for the Liberals at South Hackney in 1906 and as polling day neared he felt his campaign needed a bit of a boost. So he ordered all his horses to be sent up from their stables and then, with much ceremony, he had them paraded down Hackney High Street. On the saddle cloth of each one was emblazoned the message, 'Vote for My Owner'. The nags did the trick and the suitably impressed electors gave him a most gratifying majority.

Clara Bow (1905–1965) An actress, known somewhat ominously as the 'It' girl, who was said to have expressed her admiration for the 1927 University of Southern California football team by taking them to her bed – though presumably not all at once. The side included one Marion Morrison, a 6 foot 4 inch, 230 pound tackle who later drifted into the film world himself under the name of John Wayne. Miss Bow, meanwhile, spent the last years of her life as a respectable matron in the hinterland of Nevada.

Dr Joseph O. Boydstone The golfer who discovered the knack of holing in one. In just one calendar year the lucky old devil had 11 of them, including, on 10 October 1962, three in one day. This was when he aced the 3rd, 4th and 9th holes at Bakerfield Golf Club in California. The justice of this run of flukes can be gauged from the fact that in the whole of his life the great Harry Vardon had just one hole in one.

Arthur Boynton This American made boxing's most optimistic comeback attempt. In 1983 the 6 foot 3 inch heavyweight tried to prove to the Vermont Boxing Commission that he was fit for a return to the amateur ring. He told

CLARA BOW

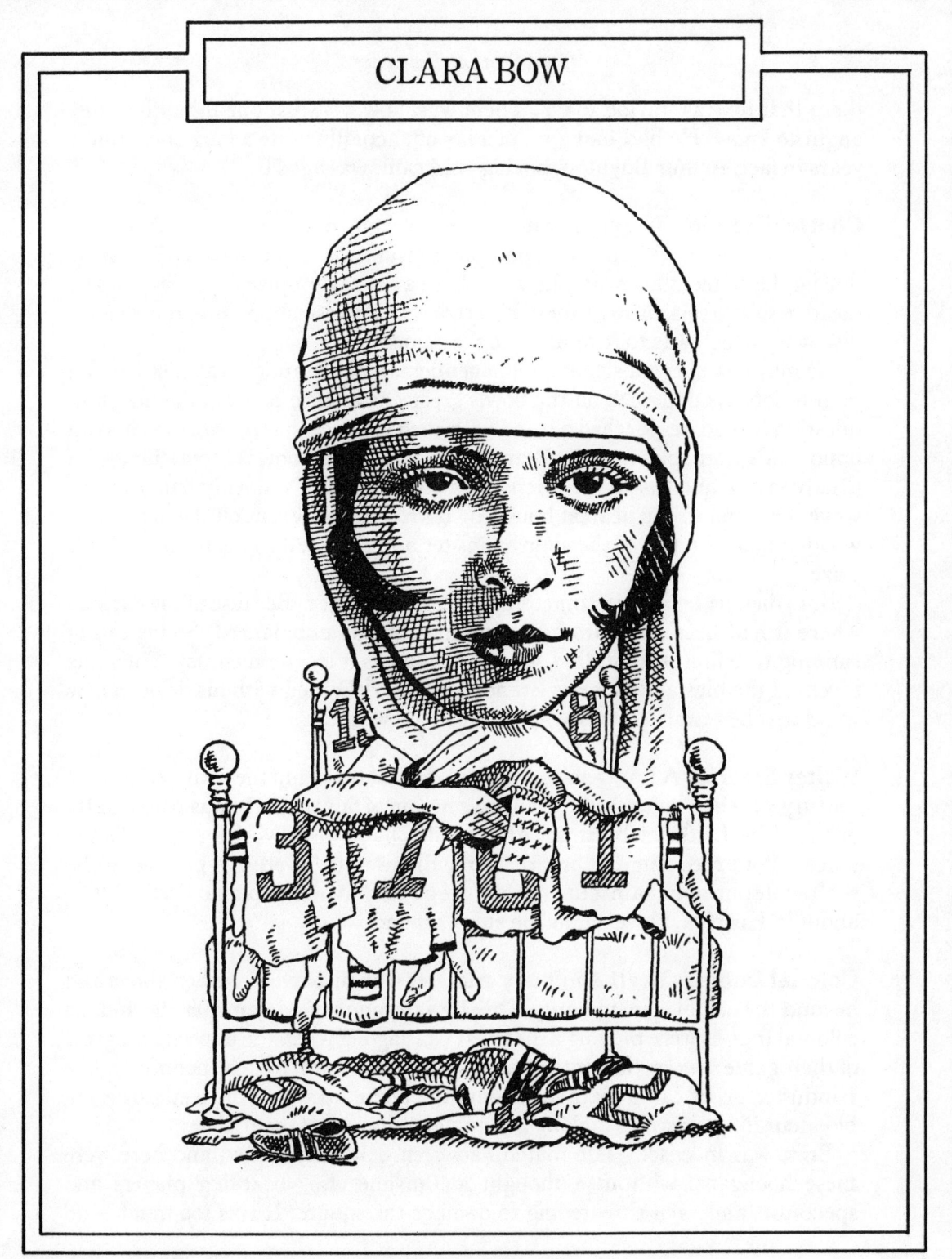

Football lover

them that he was 'raring to go'. There was, however, just one thing that they ought to know. He had had a bit of a lay off; actually quite a long one – thirty years in fact. Arthur Boynton, boxing applicant, was aged 61.

Charles Brandon The perpetrator of the only known case of hooliganism in the history of lawn bowls. In his desperation to win a match at Goole in Yorkshire during the sixteenth century, he vandalised a nearby property. But there was a positive side to this outrage, for in his act of wanton destruction Brandon made a discovery which was to revolutionise the game.

He may have been a scholar and a gentleman but Brandon was clearly not a man to fool around with on the bowls green. At a tense point in the match in question he had despatched a wood with such violence that it cannoned into an opponent's and split in two. Brandon was obviously now at something of a disadvantage and might have remained so had he not suddenly had a brainwave. Dashing to the nearest house, he borrowed a saw, cut off the decorative wooden globe on top of the stair bannister and returned to the green with his prize.

But when he bowled it, something strange happened. Because of the flat side where it had been sawn from its moorings, it was unbalanced. So instead of running true in a straight line, it curled round as it lost momentum. Thus was invented the bias and Charles Brandon was so delighted with his devious new wood that he rewarded the owner of the house with £5.

Walter Brearley A Lancashire and England fast bowler in the early years of the century who had an unusually sensitive notion of fair play. He was particularly offended by Leicester batsman Albert Hill's habit of praying for divine assistance before receiving his first delivery. Brearley believed this practice to be such a vile outrage against the spirit of the game that he complained to the MCC about it. His plea, however, fell on stony ground.

Colonel Douglas Brett A military cricketer who displayed courage above and beyond the call of sporting duty. One Indian summer's day in 1934 he and his colonial friends were playing a match at Chittagong when the imperial progress of their game was crudely interrupted. All at once from over the boundary, five Hindu terrorists came marauding onto the pitch, armed to the teeth, uttering bloodcurdling cries and making a thorough nuisance of themselves.

Brett was incensed. The match had been delicately poised and here were these hooligans, without a thought for anyone else, attacking players and spectators and even threatening to damage the square. It was too much – no

Englishman could be expected to stand idly by and watch such sacrilege. So he got stuck in, with such vigour and to such effect, that the terrorists were repulsed. A grateful nation awarded him the Empire Gallantry Medal.

Edwin Brett This late Victorian publisher founded *Jack Harkaway's Journal for Boys* to encourage what he described as 'the manly sports of Britain'. Just in case his young readers were not inspired by the lurid yarns of athletic derring-do, Brett provided an irresistible incentive. He offered £20 to the next-of-kin of any boy killed while playing football or cricket or riding a bicycle.

In fact the stories in Brett's and other papers did untold damage to the image of sport. Weaned on tales of poisoned lemons at half-time, unscrupulous rivals kidnapping star players and swarthy foreigners roaming the English countryside in search of house matches to disrupt, generations of schoolboys grew up believing that every crevice of the sporting world was infected with bribery and corruption.

Bobby Bridge (1883–1953) A Lancashire postman who, despite having his left arm amputated at the elbow, won seven Amateur Athletic Association walking titles. Even more laudable was the fact that with the aid of only one forearm and hand he then proceeded to qualify as a dentist.

Jack Broughton (1704–1789) The Father of Boxing and Champion of England for 16 years. When this bareknuckle fighter from Cirencester, Gloucestershire eventually lost the title to Slack of Bristol in April 1750, he showed a courage that bordered on the insane. Broughton had arrived for this fight with not only the hopes of his supporters, but also £10,000 of the Duke of Cumberland's money riding on his back. The Duke, known as 'The Butcher of Culloden' for his homicidal activities in the Scottish Highlands, liked to win. So when Broughton was blinded by his opponent's blows after just 14 minutes of the fight, the bloodthirsty gambler declared himself betrayed.

But the agonised prizefighter, even though he now could not see, thought the matter was far from settled. As he groped around the ring for his opponent, Broughton yelled out, 'I can't see my man your Highness. I am blind. But not beat, only place me before him and he shall yet not gain the day.' With these heroic words and Slack's swift and violent response, the title changed hands. Broughton retired, taught the 'noble art' to the aristocracy, introduced gloves for sparring and ended his days as a Yeoman of the Guard at the Tower of London. When he finally died at the ripe old age of 84 he was commemorated with a memorial in Westminster Abbey.

Ambrose Brown The possessor of the quickest temper in football. He got so worked up by the opening exchanges of the Hull v Wrexham match in December 1936 that he was sent off, after only 20 seconds.

Brian and Susan Brown A married couple from Wrottesley near Wolverhampton who were besotted with boxing. Their enthusiasm reached such a pitch that in April 1974 they named their two-month-old daughter Maria Sullivan Corbett Fitzsimmons Jeffries Hart Burns Johnson Willard Dempsey Tunney Schmeling Sharkey Carnero Baer Braddock Louis Charles Walcott Marciano Patterson Johannson Liston Clay Frazier Foreman Brown.

   Young Maria will presumably find some way of coping with being christened after every heavyweight champion of the world. Until her wedding, that is. 'I Maria Sullivan Corbett Fitzsimmons. . . .'

Mrs Dorothy Cavis Brown The most infamous lineswoman in Wimbledon history. She earned her immortality in 1964 when a ballboy found her asleep on Court No. 3. She explained later, 'I have had a very exhausting time lately.'

John Bunyan (1628–1688) The author of *Pilgrim's Progress* and, so far as is known, the only man ever to have had a vision telling him to give up hockey.

   In his youth Bunyan was a keen player of an early form of the game. He would even turn out on a Sunday, a somewhat frivolous thing to do in the seventeenth century. This must have preyed on his mind because one fateful Sunday he looked up in mid-game and saw in the sky a vast frowning face regarding him with disapproval. He was so alarmed by his celestial rebuke that he gave up the game there and then and immediately renounced 'all idle pastimes'.

Revd Robert 'Pops' Burgess (b. 1907) A New York clergyman who was still playing ice hockey at the advanced age of 77. He turned out for the New York Apple Core Oldtimers and nothing could ever deter him from his weekly game – not even the fact that the only ice-time the side got was between 11 p.m. and 2 a.m.

   So every Monday between October and April, at a time of night when most pensioners have long since taken their teeth out, the Revd Burgess would make his way to the Murray Memorial Ice Rink in Yonkers. The aged pastor was always the first to arrive since it was his job to collect the side's $8 dues. This done, he would stuff the money inside his left sock behind his shin pad, secure his glasses under his helmet and head for the ice with his tartan scarf tucked beneath his jersey. There he joined fellow lunatics like Arnie Caruso, a survivor of triple by-pass surgery, for three hours of the fastest team game in sport.

He played left wing in a version of the game (no heavy checking, boarding or slap shots) that is only marginally less lethal than the original. At the end of the session he would pay the rink attendant and was always the last to leave. Then the old man, who started playing in the early 1920s and once coached the Canadian Army side, would head back home ready in a few hours time to resume ministering to his congregation of 600 at the Bellerose Assembly of God Church in Queens.

Billy Buttress A Cambridgeshire bowler in the mid-nineteenth century, chiefly remembered for his phobic fear of batting and astonishing powers of ventriloquism.

His bowling was good enough for him to once take seven wickets for five runs against the All England XI and to be regarded as a key figure in the development of the leg break. His batting, however, was so humiliatingly poor that he often tried to avoid the experience altogether. Once, when it was his time to bat, he sought sanctuary half way up a tree. Alas he was located and his team-mates soon gathered round the trunk to remonstrate with him. But Buttress was unmoved. From his perch among the leafy boughs he yelled down, 'What's the good of me goin' in? If I miss 'em I'm out and if I hit 'em I'm out. Let's start the next innings.' And so they did.

His constant travelling companion was a stuffed kitten which, combined with his great gift for ventriloquism, provided no end of fun at the expense of unsuspecting strangers. He would conceal the animal in his baggage or under a railway carriage seat. Then when fellow passengers, preferably elderly ones, entered his compartment, he would begin emitting the most violent miaowing through his immobile lips. The other passengers would then start a search for the poor trapped creature that was making these plaintive sounds while Buttress sat there feigning indifference. Minutes later this charade would be concluded, to Buttress's immense satisfaction, with the shocked discovery of the utterly stiff and stone cold kitten.

This most worthwhile of human beings died from a surfeit of drink aged only 41.

Lord Byron (1788–1824) He may have had a lifelong tendency to obesity and been born with a club foot so deformed that he once pleaded with a doctor to amputate it, but Lord Byron was completely devoted to his sport. He played cricket at Lord's, sparred with the boxing champion of England and was one of the finest long-distance swimmers of his generation. He also wrote some poetry

LORD BYRON

Cricketer, pugilist and conqueror of the Hellespont

and was an accomplished debauchee.

His appearance at the inaugural Eton v Harrow cricket match was an early triumph over his disabilities. In childhood his club foot had received the painful attentions of every quack in the land including, of all people, the truss maker to Nottingham Infirmary. He somehow survived and by his final year at Eton was fit enough to lead a mutiny against the new headmaster and play at Lord's. He went to the wicket with a runner and scored seven in the first innings and two in the second. Intriguingly he was listed in the batting order after a boy named Shakespeare.

By this time, however, his weight was becoming a heavy burden. When he went up to Cambridge at 17 years of age the 5 foot 8 inch undergraduate tipped the scales at 16 stone. He tried to lose unwanted pounds by playing cricket in seven waistcoats and a greatcoat but to no avail. Only when he applied himself to a rigid diet of hard biscuits and rice, washed down by soda water or diluted wine, did he assume anything like a normal shape.

But whatever the size of his waistline, he remained a strong and courageous swimmer all his life and in 1810 his prowess in the water brought him his proudest moment. On 3 May he swam the treacherous, tide-swept Hellespont Straits that divide Europe and Asia. He made the 1¼ mile crossing in one hour, ten minutes and was elated. Two months later he wrote, 'I plume myself on this achievement more than I could possibly do on any kind of glory, political, poetical or rhetorical.' No sports nut could ever have put it better.

C

Sir Julien Cahn (1882–1944) A millionaire upholsterer who was so enraptured with cricket that he employed his own private team, built a lavish ground for their exclusive use and sent several touring teams abroad. His love of the game was said to cost him £20,000 a year. Sir Julien also had a second ground laid out at his home near Loughborough and it was here that he himself played. Sadly for such an enthusiast his lack of ability bordered on the comic, an effect which he unwittingly emphasised by always batting in inflatable pads.

Caligula Roman Emperor and pervert he may have been, but in a lifetime devoted to unprintable sexual practices he always found time for a good chariot race. His meetings at the Circus Maximus went on from dawn to dusk and he was a frequent and keen competitor. Caligula, however, liked to win and the evening before the races he would send his soldiers out to enforce silence in the neighbourhood of the stables so that his horses could have a good night's rest. If he had treated his women half as well, history might have been different.

Albert Camus (1913–1960) Novelist, Nobel Prize winner and goalkeeper for the Oran Football Club in Algiers. His regard for the game was so high that he once wrote, 'All that I know surely about morality and the obligations of man, I owe to football.'

Thomas J. Caradonio This American golf enthusiast wanted to make sure that when he entered eternity he would be properly equipped. So he stipulated in his will that on his death he should be laid to rest wearing his golf clothes, spiked shoes and holding his putter in his hands. In the event his instructions were easily obeyed, for one weekend in August 1984 he holed out on the 8th green at the Willowisp Country Club in Houston, Texas, suffered a heart attack and died – all dressed up and ready for his burial.

Felix Carvajal A Cuban postman and possibly the most accident-prone marathon entrant in Olympic history. The troubles of this little five foot mailman began even before he had arrived at the 1904 St Louis Games. On the boat trip to the United States his luggage was stolen and then he lost all his money in a dice game. When he landed in New Orleans he had to hitch a ride to St Louis and by the time he arrived the only possessions he had were the clothes that hung on his back.

So when the runners assembled at the marathon starting line one bedraggled little figure stood out. All the field were in singlets and shorts, except one. Felix Carvajal, poised ready for the greatest challenge in athletics, wore a beret, multi-coloured shirt, long cotton trousers and street shoes. He looked like an onion seller without his bicycle. This bizarre apparition was greeted with general derision and merriment until a sympathetic soul, American discus thrower Martin Sheridan, borrowed a pair of scissors and gave Carvajal a more athletic-looking appearance by cutting off his sleeves at the elbow and his trousers at the knee.

When the race began the Cuban raced off in his newly ventilated attire, ran well and with a few miles to go was in with a chance. Then he saw an orchard. The temptation was too much and he went in and gorged himself on apples and peaches. His scrumping might not have mattered if the fruit had been ripe, but it wasn't, and after having spent some uncomfortable moments doubled up behind a hedge, Carvajal eventually trailed in an agonised fourth.

Hugh Case An early football martyr. In 1589 he and William Shurlock were fined two shillings for playing the game. The fact that they chose as a pitch the cemetery of St Werburgh's Church, Chester and kicked off during the vicar's sermon may have had something to do with it. This pair were lucky, at least they got a game. In 1610 two men were prosecuted and fined at Bedford merely for watching football on a Sunday.

John Graham Chambers (1843–1883) The one-man sporting bureaucracy. In a brief period towards the end of the nineteenth century he wrote the Queensbury Rules for boxing, re-wrote the rules for billiards, founded the Inter-Varsity sports, staged the FA Cup Final and the Thames Regatta, managed Lillie Bridge Stadium and started national championships for billiards, boxing, cycling, wrestling and athletics.

Earlier, at Cambridge, he was president of the university boat club and modernised athletics by introducing shot-putting and hammer throwing in place of 'toy' events like the sack race and pole jump. Chambers also won the Amateur Athletics Club seven miles walk, coached Cambridge to four successive Boat Race victories and rowed beside Captain Webb on his famous Channel swim. He somehow found time to earn his living as editor of the *Land and Water* newspaper. Not surprisingly he died worn out aged only 40.

Sir Claude Champion Throughout his life this outrageous nineteenth century sportsman accepted challenges that even seasoned maniacs refused to contemplate. At the age of 42 he became the first European to swim the Nile Rapids, in 1883 he and a partner made the first balloon crossing of the North Sea, at 61 he walked 45 miles from Essex to London for a bet of 2s 6d and until well into his sixties he was still riding steeplechases.

His sporting obsessions even extended to the hiring of staff. Sir Claude believed boxing to be such an infallible test of man's character that anyone who applied to work at his large country house had to go several rounds with him. This engaging specimen also once claimed to be the war correspondent of *The Sporting Times*.

Earl of Chesterfield (1694–1773) A rascally old aristocrat who so detested the Turf that he inserted a clause in his will prohibiting his heir from having anything to do with horse racing.

The full terms read, 'In case my godson Philip Stanhope shall at anytime keep or be concerned in keeping any racehorse or pack of hounds, or reside one night at Newmarket, that infamous seminary of iniquity and ill-manners, during the course of the races there, or shall resort to the said races or shall lose in one day at any game or bet whatsoever the sum of £500 then in any of the cases aforesaid, it is my express will that he, my said godson, shall forfeit and pay out of my estate the sum of £50,000 to and for the use of the Dean and Chapter of Westminster.'

Nor, as the family solicitor would have added, is that all. As well as keeping off the racecourse, 'He was by no means to go into Italy . . . the foul sink of illiberal manners and vices.' This last clause was a bit rich since its author was not noted for his restraint and kept mistresses and gambled freely in the London clubs. He had perhaps undergone some late-life crisis because his will also stipulated a frugal funeral. The expenses were not to exceed £100 and the Earl was to be interred in the nearest graveyard to where he had died.

The beneficiary of this extraordinary document by and large stuck to its terms but its influence in the family was short-lived. The following Lord Chesterfield had a voracious passion for racing and his horses won the St Leger in 1838 and the Oaks in 1849.

Vicar of Chipstead This Wiltshire clergyman was so anxious to encourage the playing of cricket in his village that he allowed the local team to use the church vestry as a pavilion and to take the hymn board outside as a scoreboard.

Dong-Kih Choh A South Korean flyweight who brought the 1964 Olympic boxing tournament to a halt. The trouble came in the first round of his opening bout when he threw a punch after the referee called 'stop' and was then disqualified. He so resented this that he refused to leave the ring until the referee's decision had been reversed. Just to emphasise the point he sat down in the middle of the canvas and would not budge.

At first the officials tried to reason with him. They told him not to be such a silly lad and asked him what he thought his dear old mother would say if she knew. But he just sat there and ten minutes went by. Then they started to plead with him and pointed out what a scene he was making and asked him to consider all the other boxers waiting to fight. It was no use, Dong-Kih remained rooted to the spot. As 20 minutes became half an hour, a few threats started to slip out. Had he heard of 'disciplinary measures' and did he know what 'life ban' meant? Still he sat there unmoved. When 40 minutes ticked by, a pair of officials could stand it no longer. Grabbing hold of a couple of his limbs each, they tried to remove the Korean by force. All to no avail, for the dogged Dong-Kih just sat tight.

Finally the officials played their last desperate card: they offered him an inquiry into the referee's decision. It did the trick. With the greatest reluctance and after occupying the ring for 50 minutes, the South Korean left. Quite what his national team manager said to him is not known. What is certain is that he was never seen at the Olympics again.

Winston Spencer Churchill Representing Harrow he won the Public Schools Foil Championships in 1892 and as a junior boy he had the honour and privilege to fag for future England cricket captain, F.S. Jackson. Sporting old Harrovians often wondered what became of him in later life.

A.H.S. Clark The least effective cricketer in the history of the county

Swordsman and statesman

championship. In nine successive innings for Somerset in 1929 he scored 0,0,0,0,0,0,0,0 and 0. What made the sequence harder to bear was that it was his entire first class career, surely one of the most futile appearances ever made on the sporting stage.

Mrs Iris Clarke The cause, in 1983, of cricket's only known case of 'angry old lady stopped play'. The hold-up came in a match between Hampshire 2nd XI and a Southern League side when batsman Robin Smith hit a ball through the window of her flat overlooking the Southampton ground.

Mrs Clarke was furious and decided that something had to be done. So she left her flat, stomped onto the pitch and refused to leave until she had told the players exactly what she thought of them. The players, hoping she would go away if they said nothing, merely smirked and smiled. This was a mistake. Mrs Clarke said they were being silly and she didn't think it was funny at all and just to show them she jolly well wasn't going to give them their ball back. They said she was holding up their game and the spectators were getting restless and would she please mind leaving the field. She replied that if they could break her windows, she could spoil their cricket and what did they think about that?

Finally, all such avenues of debate having been explored and her indignation being spent, Mrs Clark subsided back beyond the boundary, disappeared off to her flat and play resumed.

Roger Coates Scoring a century before tea is common, recording one before lunch is by no means unknown, but this Cambridge undergraduate made a hundred before breakfast. It came in a 24-hour cricket match played on Parker's Piece, Cambridge in June 1973. Play began at 5 p.m. and proceeded under the usual rules except that no fast bowling was allowed during the hours of darkness. Assisted by these rather favourable circumstances Coates went to the wicket at 1.43 a.m. and, batting by the light of the moon, four street lamps and two gas arc lights, he compiled his nocturnal century.

William J. Cobb (b. 1926) An American wrestler whose size fluctuated alarmingly. In one ten year period he lost and gained 70 stone, the equivalent of the weight of six average men. He fought under the name of 'Happy Humphrey' and in the early 1960s he would enter the ring weighing a juddering 57 stone 4 pounds. At this weight entering the ring was no easy matter and he decided to slim down. In the course of the next three years he shed layer after layer until he had finally shrunk to 16 stone 8 pounds. With his waist measurement reduced from 8 foot 5 inches to a sylph-like 44 inches, he was now a mere shadow of his former self. Sad to say, a certain amount of backsliding set in and his weight started to go up again. By October 1973 he was back to a 'normal' size of 46 stone 7 pounds.

S.F. Cody In 1903 this ingenious man made a most civilised crossing of the English Channel. Settling into a small boat, he sat back, operated the tiller and enjoyed the passing scene as a 15 foot kite towed him all the way to France. The journey took him 13 hours.

Edward Colbeck A Victorian athlete who broke a leg and the world 440 yards record in the same race. Fortunately the limb was not on his own. It belonged instead to a sheep which had wandered onto the running track at Beaufort House during the running of the quarter mile event at the Amateur Athletic Club's championships in 1868. As Colbeck rounded the bend at full-tilt he collided with the animal and broke its leg but still managed to set a new world best time of 50.4 seconds. The record stood for 11 years which, sadly, is more than can be said for the sheep.

Arthur Coningham (1863–1939) Never did a man lead a life that was such an absurd mixture of sporting triumph and domestic disaster. He played cricket for Queensland and Australia, set records at that game and athletics, excelled in at least four other sports and was a good enough swimmer to once rescue a drowning boy from the River Thames. Yet when he finally left the sports field, chaos was always liable to ensue. His attempt to end his marriage ended in a public fiasco, he brawled with a priest in a courtroom and, by way of an encore, served a prison sentence for fraud. After all this, it seems only fitting that he should have ended his days in a Sydney mental home.

Coningham was born in Melbourne the son of a brass finisher and he was barely out of his teens when he established himself as an outstanding athlete. He went into the record books as a sprinter and a hurdler, won titles at shooting and was a distinguished oarsman, billiards and rugby player. As a cricketer he was a brilliant slip field and skilled all-rounder who seemed to have a knack for the eye-catching performance. In 1891, playing for Stanley C.C. against Albert C.C., he scored every run of his side's entire total of 26, he was the first man to score a century for Queensland and on 29 December 1894 he took a wicket with his first ever ball in Test cricket. Even when not directly involved in the action he was capable of causing a stir, as at Lord's during the 1893 tour. While fielding in the deep he found the weather distinctly chilly and to draw attention to this, he gathered some twigs, lit a small fire and ostentatiously warmed himself.

When he retired from the game in 1899 he put his reputation to good use by setting up as a bookie on Randwick racetrack with a bag inscribed 'Coningham the Cricketer'. But he had not been shouting the odds there for long when the domestic turbulence that was to shadow the rest of his life began. The seeds had been sown in 1893 with his strange decision to marry just a matter of hours before he and the rest of the Australian cricket team left on the boat to tour England. A four month separation was hardly an ideal preparation for connubial bliss and the marriage foundered in spectacular style. Six years after the hurried ceremony Coningham tried to divorce his wife Alice in a case still celebrated as one of the most farcical lawsuits of all time.

The proceedings had everything. Coningham cited a Catholic priest as co-respondent, named the unfortunate Father D.F. O'Haran as the father of his wife's youngest child and claimed £5,000 damages. Spurning professional help, he conducted his own case and left no detail of his bizarre marriage unexplored. He even called a doctor to give evidence that he could not have fathered the disputed child because of 'an injury from a cricket ball he had received'.

After an inconclusive hearing a re-trial was ordered. Here passions reached such a height that at one point Coningham had to be relieved of a revolver in the courtroom. When it was announced that the jury had dismissed the case he hurled himself at the poor priest, sending court furniture and assorted legal gentlemen flying as he wrestled with those restraining him. The aftermath of this action was no less eventful. He managed to effect some kind of reconciliation with Alice, took his family to New Zealand, worked as a book salesman and was then jailed for six months after being caught fraudulently converting. He and his wife were finally divorced in 1912 after the discovery of his adultery in the cramped surroundings of a beach hut. Eventually life's little adventures took their toll and in 1937 'Coningham the Cricketer' was admitted to Ryde Mental Home in Sydney where he died two years later.

James Connolly When this American academic asked for leave of absence to compete at the 1896 Olympics, the Dean of Harvard, where he worked, refused even to consider the matter. Connolly's response was to walk out of Harvard and a promising university career and travel to Athens for the Games. His reward, on 6 April, was to become the first Olympic champion of the modern era by winning the triple jump with a leap of 44 foot 11¾ inches. After the Games he turned to writing and his first novel *Out of Gloucester* was published in 1902. He later became a distinguished war correspondent for *Collier's Magazine*.

Ernest Connor At the start of the 1980 New York Marathon the eyes of every one of the 15,000 or so entrants were fixed on the road ahead. All except one pair, that is, for Ernest Connor was looking at the road behind. He stayed like that all the way to the finish and ran the entire 26 miles 385 yards backwards in a time of 5 hours 18 minutes.

Controller of Rubber Wartime bureaucrat who ensured that Britain's golfers would have sufficient ammunition throughout the Second World War. In 1942 he had caused widespread alarm in the game by banning the remould of old golf balls. His office was deluged with protests and the Controller, given this reminder of our sporting heritage, allowed wiser counsels to prevail. Only in Britain could the war effort have included balls on its agenda.

William Cook An obstinate left back, he single-handedly caused the abandonment of a First Division football game 35 minutes from time. He was playing for Oldham against Middlesborough on 3 April 1915 when he committed such a gross foul that even in those far from squeamish times he was immediately sent off. Thinking the referee an untutored oaf who had completely misconstrued his attempt to play the ball, Cook refused to leave the field. When all efforts at persuasion had failed, the referee called off the match there and then with Middlesborough leading 4-1. The League ordered the result to stand and Cook was suspended for a year.

Peter Corrigan A Welsh golf fanatic whose attempts to start his club's Sunday morning competition resulted in the calling out of the Penarth and Barry lifeboats on a full-scale coastal alert. It was, to say the least, a considerable achievement and one made possible only by the devastating combination of the course's proximity to the sea and Corrigan's eagerness to get the event under way.

The unhappy tale unfolded at the Glamorganshire Golf Club where Corrigan was the man in charge of the winter foursomes tournament. He decided that the best way to set this contest in motion was for all 144 golfers to distribute themselves around the 18 tees and stand ready to play at a given signal. The problem was, what kind of signal? Previous attempts with an air-horn had failed when it was heard by only half the competitors, whereas the local yacht club cannon, resourcefully scrounged by Corrigan, was heard so well that it brought complaints from nearby residents. So, the course being near the sea and sailing clubs abounding, he opted on this occasion for a flare and at 9 a.m. on 4 March 1984, with eight golfers waiting like greyhounds in a trap at each tee, Corrigan triggered the device and the players were off.

And not only the players. For when Mrs Beryl Thomas saw the flare from some distance away she was also off – in the direction of the nearest telephone. She knew a maroon when she saw one and naturally she assumed the worst. Even now, she thought, the poor devil who fired the distress signal is probably sinking beneath the waves. She hurriedly dialled the police who contacted the coastguard and thus was set in motion a full-scale in-shore rescue operation.

Within minutes lifeboatmen were running from their homes to launch their vessel. The Barry Docks lifeboat, already at sea on an exercise, was ordered to join the search and for 20 minutes they scanned the sea for non-existent survivors. Then, just as they were beginning to abandon hope, came the news from the Swansea coastguard that a golf club had claimed responsibility for the flare and the phantom alert was called off. Several hours later, as Corrigan came off the 18th green glowing with pride at such a smoothly run golf competition, there to greet him were a policeman and the duty lifeboat officer. The club now uses white flares.

Arthur Courcy The 1882 Oval Test against Australia, which England lost by just seven runs, was one of the most agonisingly close matches in the history of the contest. During England's second innings, Courcy, an Epsom stockbroker, found the tension of 12 successive maiden overs so unbearable that he gnawed through the handle of his brother-in-law's umbrella while watching them. Only a single from the bat of the Hon. Alfred Lyttleton prevented further damage to the borrowed implement.

Bucky Cox A Texan infant who defied all known medical advice and ran a marathon at the appallingly precocious age of five. Her time was 5 hours 29 minutes and two years later, in 1980, she improved this to 3 hours 40 minutes.

Albert Craig (1849–1909) Sporting poet and the self-styled 'captain of the crowd' at many a Victorian and Edwardian cricket and football match. At an FA Cup tie in 1908 he was instrumental in averting a pitch invasion. The crowd was furious at a refereeing decision and began to break out from the terraces. But suddenly Craig's voice roared out from among the throng, 'Boys, do nothing tonight that you will regret tomorrow. I have been your captain for 20 years, so take my advice and go home.' They obeyed and a grateful Chelsea sent him a letter of thanks. It is not, however, a method of crowd control that could be safely imitated today.

Craig earnt his living by selling topical sporting verses of his own composition at cricket grounds up and down the country. With titles like *Young Jack Hobbs to the Rescue* and *Kent Full of Hope For the Future*, these poems were a collation of clichés served with the tug of a deferential forelock. Always signed 'A.C. Cricket Rhymster', they were firmly in the mainstream of the greetings card school of verse writing. One sample, but a fragment of an epic entitled *First Prize Rhyme on the Game of Cricket* and addressed to the captain of Kent, Lord Harris, will illustrate why Craig's works are not more widely quoted –

> 'Your brilliant deed was but a repetition
> Of former triumphs 'gainst Colonial teams.
> You were, my Lord, in extra fine condition –
> Kent did their duty; so at least it seems,
> 'Twas no mere fluke – on conquering you were bent;
> You did it by ten wickets; bravo! Kent.'

Craig himself was under no delusion about the quality of his work. At Canterbury Week in 1890, as he touted his masterpiece around the ground, he cried, 'I know that any fool among you could write a better poem than this, but I defy anyone else, however intelligent, to sell it at 2d a copy.'

Revd J.C. Crawford The chaplain to Cane Hill lunatic asylum in Surrey and most definitely cricket mad. He could bat and bowl with either hand, played for Kent and Leicestershire and turned out for the MCC against Whitgift School at the age of 76. His most bizarre act was to be the sole objector to a 1902 MCC motion that the bowling crease be extended from 78 inches to 80 inches and yet refuse to give his reasons to the chairman.

He also sired three of the greatest cricket prodigies of all time, plus a daughter, Lesley, who once scored a century for Woodmansterne C.C. His eldest son Vivian was in the local club side at eight, the Whitgift School 1st XI at 13 and was a stupendous hitter of the ball. At 17, playing for Young Amateurs of Surrey v Young Professionals, he scored a double century before lunch. He also once took a century off a club attack in 19 minutes and at the Oval, off the bowling of Wilfred Rhodes, smacked a fierce, low drive that laid out a watching parson first bounce.

Despite a club foot, the middle son R.T. Crawford was playing for Leicestershire by the age of 19. But he was an accomplished singer and his stage and concert engagements soon put paid to his cricket. The greatest of them all, however, was Jack who in 1905, in true *Boy's Own Paper* style, went straight from the school team into the England side. He had a brief but colourful county and Test career before emigrating to Australia where he once helped Victor Trumper put on 298 in 69 minutes for South Australia. But, like all the

Crawford boys, his glory was in his youth and none of them could match their father's lengthy years of activity.

Brigadier General Critchley The efforts that this military man made to play in the 1937 Amateur Golf Championship were positively heroic. Some weeks before the event he had been in America and although he managed to leave New York in good time to cross the Atlantic, he soon ran into trouble. The Queen Mary was held up by fog and arrived at Southampton just a few hours before the Brigadier General was due to start his round, 140 miles away.

The position seemed hopeless. But Critchley was undaunted, he had got out of tighter spots in the past and was determined to do so again now. So he telephoned the organisers to let them know that he was on his way and then chartered a plane to fly across Southern England to the championship venue at Sandwich in Kent. As the plane approached the course it circled over the clubhouse, dipping a wing to let the officials inside know that its cargo would soon be with them. After a landing in a nearby field, Critchley dashed to the first tee. He was six minutes late and therefore disqualified.

Revd Ben Crockett A football-mad clergyman who declined to marry a couple because the ceremony clashed with a Derby County home match. The Revd Crockett, vicar of All Saints, Mickleover, had been a season ticket holder at the Baseball Ground for 20 years and as he said himself, 'It has long been my policy not to marry couples after 1 p.m. on Saturdays when Derby are at home.' So when bride-to-be Helen Warner and her fiancé Robert Madeley came to him and named the happy day as 13 October 1984 at 3.30 p.m., the sporting parson said he would have to wait until the football fixtures were published before he knew whether he could conduct their service. Unluckily for the young couple, the Football League also named 13 October as the day when County would entertain Plymouth Argyle. A marriage at All Saints was therefore out of the question.

Miss Warner, who had attended the church since she was four and had set her heart on marrying there, was furious and she complained not only to the Bishop of Derby but also to the Archbishop of Canterbury. She said, 'They say God's house is always open but in this case only if Derby are playing away.' The 70-year-old Revd Crockett was unrepentant and on 13 October, while the young lovers plighted their troth at Aston-on-Trent, he took his usual seat in the Derby stands and watched his favourite team win 3-1.

D

Derek Dalton Probably the most dedicated football fan in Britain. He contracted polio at the age of two in 1949 but despite being so severely disabled that he has had to spend a large part of his life on his back, Dalton has given Rotherham United fanatical support for 30 years. He travels about 5,000 miles a season following his favourite team in a specially equipped van, is a life president of Rotherham Supporters' Club, a member of the players' testimonial committee, shareholder, fundraiser and a lotteries agent.

Hugh Daly Between 1882 and 1887 this American played second base and pitched for several major baseball teams. He also set a new record for striking out 19 batters in a game; all of which is not bad for a man with only one arm.

Walter Danecki In middle age this mail-sorter from Milwaukee developed a burning desire to become a golf professional. The fact that he was not much good at the game and had never been a member of a golf club or even a driving range did not worry him and he duly applied to the United States Professional Golfers' Association for membership. The response from that august body was not encouraging. After all, 43 was rather an advanced age for him to embark on the five year apprenticeship that they required.

Very well then, Danecki said to himself, if he could not get into this exclusive club by the tradesman's entrance, he would march boldly in through the front door. He would go out and win one of the world's major golf championships. 'Then they'll have to let me in,' he said. Since there seemed no point in mucking around with anything less than the best, he duly sent in his entry for the 1965 Open Championship. Admittedly he told a few fibs when he filled out the application form but he was accepted and come that July he took a break from mail-sorting and crossed the Atlantic for the qualifying round at Hillside in Lancashire.

His first round certainly made the world of golf sit up and take notice. After all, it is not every day that a player in the Open shoots a round of 108. But unrestrained mirth was not quite the effect he had intended and to the mailman who had set his heart on winning golf's biggest prize, a score of 38 over par represented something of a disappointment. Anyone else would have slunk off into the night before too many questions were asked, but not Danecki and the following morning there he was on the first tee, bright-eyed and raring to go. What he needed was a nice steady start and he got it with a pair of sevens at the opening two holes. He was consistency itself and only a momentary lapse at the third, where he took eight, prevented him maintaining his momentum.

Then, tragically, he began to crack under the pressure of playing in a major championship. A nine at the seventh and another one at the tenth were sure signs that nerves were unsettling his game. In normal circumstances both those holes would have been elementary par sevens to Danecki but now all his usual rhythm and assurance was gone. At the twelfth, which looked on the card to be a sure-fire eight, he took a ten. Everything was going haywire. He became so rattled that he even scored two fours in the home stretch. Eventually he reeled off the 18th green with a score of 113 and a two-round aggregate of 221 – no fewer than 70 shots over the qualifying mark.

In the interview afterwards he was philosophical. 'I want to say that your smaller ball is right for this kind of course. If I had been playing a bigger ball I would have been all over the place.' He also had a confession to make. On the application form he had put himself down as a professional but, lest anyone think that he had been taking money under false pretences, he quickly added, 'I don't charge if I give a lesson.'

Joe Darby (1861–1937) A lively little individual, he jumped clean over a billiard table at a hall in Wolverhampton on 5 February 1892. Taking off from a four inch block of wood, he generated sufficient momentum to clear the 2 foot 10 inch high, 12 foot long table and land the other end. Quite why he did it remains a mystery.

John Davis The leader of Britain's first sporting team to tour abroad. On his first trip to Greenland this sixteenth century explorer had noted that the

Eskimos were great games enthusiasts. So when he set sail for a second time in 1586, he took a company of athletes with him to the Arctic Circle. Once there he arranged a series of sports contests to win over the suspicious natives.

From what little that has come down to us by way or results, it appears that we won the jumping, lost the wrestling and rather routed them at football. It is hard to say why the Eskimos lost so heavily – an unfamiliarity with the rules perhaps, or it may have been their close season. Either way, they have shunned international sport ever since.

Walter Davis Perhaps the most unlikely Olympic gold medallist ever. At the age of eight he was struck down by polio and when he had recovered from its worst ravages he still had to spend five years in a wheelchair. Even up to a few years before his appearance at the Games he had been unable to walk without crutches. Yet when he was at last able to get about unaided he trained so assiduously that he went to the 1952 Helsinki Olympics and won the gold medal in, of all events, the high jump.

Dan Dawson (1765–1812) The most enthusiastic nobbler of racehorses ever to cast his shadow upon the Turf. He was always a fairly deadly dispenser of dope but in May 1811 he excelled himself. He was hired by two well-known race fixers, Joe and Jim Bland, to get at a string of horses trained at Newmarket by Richard Prince. Dawson was determined to do a thorough job and so bought some arsenic and put it in a water trough on Newmarket Heath from which the horses always drank during their gallops. Unfortunately he rather overdid the doseage, tipping in six ounces of the poison, enough to kill over 1,300 people. The result, not surprisingly, was that not only were the horses slowed up but four of them died, including Sir Frank Standish's Eagle, and numerous others were taken ill.

This level of carnage scandalised even the roughest elements of the racing world and Dawson was forced to go on the run. The *Racing Calendar*, not a journal normally noted for its high moral tone, offered a reward of 500 guineas leading to a conviction. Sure enough, this drew from out of the woodwork one Cecil Bishop, a chemist, and when Dawson was tried on the charge of killing Eagle, Bishop gave evidence that he had sold him the arsenic for this and other poisonings. After Dawson was convicted and sentenced to death the Blands visited him in prison nearly every day, securing his silence by constantly assuring him that a reprieve was on it way. They were still assuring him on 8 August 1812 but shortly after their comforting visit that day, Dawson was taken out and hung in front of a crowd of 12,000.

Joe Deakin (b. 1879) This seemingly inexhaustible athlete had a competitive running career which spanned no fewer than 82 years. He ran his first race at the age of eight in 1887 and he was still appearing in the Surrey Athletic Club winter handicap event right up to his 90th birthday in 1969. In between he won many titles, including the Irish mile and four mile championships in 1901 and the Olympic three mile team event in 1908.

Harry Dearth A popular singer at the turn of the century, he once played a round of golf in a full suit of armour. In spite of this handicap he only lost the match, at Bushey Hall Golf Club, by the slender margin of 2 and 1, a result which suggests his opponent was somewhat distracted.

François Demarquette For various reasons skiing has never been an activity readily associated with the Home Counties during a summer heatwave. The lack of a decent mountain range and inadequate snowfalls have rather discouraged the sport's enthusiasts. Except, that is, for François Demarquette. One July day in 1975 he equipped his skis with a set of wheels and set out along the Thames Valley in search of a suitable piste. At last he found it and fixing a rope to the back of a car driven by his wife, took the strain and prepared himself for a little gentle slalom.

It was at this point that things went wrong. Now the M4 motorway is an excellent place for many things – nipping down to the West Country, for instance, or seeing how fast the car can go before the speedometer needle flies off – but in the opinion of the police who passed him in full cry on the hard shoulder, weaving along on wheeled skis at the end of a tow-rope is not one of them. Demarquette and his wife were fined £25, their driving licences were endorsed and an interesting little experiment was over.

Dan Dempsey This Australian added a new dimension to Rugby League's proud tradition of senseless physical violence. Early on in a particularly ill-natured international match against England in 1932 he broke his arm. He left the field to have the bone set and then returned to the touchline to savour the remaining thuggery at close quarters. As he watched, Dempsey realised that even in his incapacitated state a little unpleasantness was not out of the question. So he tore off his bandages, threw away his splint and rejoined the fray. His last words as he ran onto the pitch, his broken limb flapping at his side, were, 'At least I can get in someone's way.'

Mr Dench Caution was the watchword of this rather nervous little cricketer of the 1820s. For when fielding to George Brown, a ferocious and somewhat wayward bowler from Brighton, Dench would only agree to stand at long-stop if his person was protected by a sack of straw tied to his chest.

2nd Battalion, the Derbyshire regiment On 12 August 1889 at Jubbulpore, India, two companies of this battalion staged what was probably the world's most tedious sporting event. So well matched were they in muscle and lack of guile that their tug-of-war contest lasted no less that 2 hours 41 minutes. During this absurd length of time the winning team, 'H' Company, moved a net distance of only four yards, giving them an average speed of just 0.00084 mph.

Lord Desborough (1855–1945) A scarcely credible human being who was every ninteenth century adventure book hero rolled into one. But no writer would ever have dared invent a single character who could play cricket for Harrow, win a double blue at Oxford, swim Niagara Falls, climb the Matterhorn, row the Channel, bag a tiger and fight off the fuzzy-wuzzy singlehanded. Yet Desborough did all these things and more. He also did most of them while serving in Parliament, championing a variety of causes and raising a family on his large country estates.

In appearance he looked as if he had stepped straight from the pages of the *Strand* magazine. With his proud patrician head, black moustache and barrel chest he was, at well over six foot, every inch the Victorian sportsman. His attitudes, too, were perfect for the role, almost parodying those of the gentleman amateur. He excelled without apparent effort, believed training to be a species of cheating and would countenance no praise for his actions. Sport for Desborough was simply a source of enjoyment and an outlet for his prodigious energy.

This first emerged at Harrow where he twice played against Eton at Lord's and set a record for the school mile of 4 minutes 37 seconds that lasted for 60 years. At Oxford he won blue at athletics and rowing, where he stroked the boat that deadheated with Cambridge in 1877 and won by ten lengths a year later. He was president of both sports and also master of the university drag-hounds.

When he came down from Oxford his achievements were on an heroic scale. He rowed at Henley as an MP, stroked an Oxford crew across the Channel to France in 4 hours 22 minutes, climbed the Matterhorn three times by different routes in successive summer vacations, won the Punting Championship of the Thames three years in succession before retiring undefeated in 1890, rowed with two others from London to Oxford in a single day, fenced for Britain at the Olympics at the age of 50, was a superb shot and hunted big game all over the globe from Florida to India, Africa to the Rockies.

His single most absurd escapade concerned the Niagara Falls, those treacherous, swirling waters that had claimed the life in 1883 of the legendary Channel swimmer Captain Webb. Desborough had swum the Falls first in 1884 but when he visited the scene of his unheralded triumph four years later, he found that the locals refused to believe that the feat could be done. So he repeated the swim in a snowstorm. That night he wrote home to his wife, 'It was an awful day and blowing half a gale which made it worse for swimming but I had to do it . . . I hope you will not think me a beast for doing it but I don't call it risky really.' It was the authentic voice of the Boys' Own Hero.

None of these performances were the actions of a gentleman professionally at leisure. They were in fact the sporting punctuations to a life of service in the grand Victorian manner. He was elected four times as a Member of Parliament (as befits an all-rounder, twice as a Liberal, twice as a Conservative), was private secretary to the Chancellor of the Exchequer, served as Mayor of Maidenhead, tended his 3,000 acre estates at Taplow in Buckinghamshire, was a devoted father to his five children, joined the Bucks Volunteers for the Boer war and once, while serving as a special correspondent in the Snakin campaign in the Sudan, was at one point left to confront the advancing enemy alone, armed only with an umbrella.

He survived to be raised to the peerage in 1905, a signal for some to cease active life but for Desborough to begin afresh. He was made chairman of the British Olympic Association, organised the 1908 London Games and went on to become President of the MCC, Lawn Tennis Association, Amateur Athletic Association, Amateur Fencing Association, National Amateur Wrestling Association, Four-in-Hand Driving Club and the Coaching Club. He was also instrumental in setting up the Channel Swimming Association in 1925.

Nor were his interests confined to games. He was President of the London Chamber of Commerce, Imperial Chamber of Commerce, Royal Agricultural Society, Volunteer Defence Force, Chancellor of the Primrose League, Chairman of the Thames Conservancy Board for 32 years, administered a naval hospital during the Great War and chaired a Home Office committee on the police. He was said at one time to be serving on no fewer than 117 different committees. On 9 January 1945 he died. Today, in the age of the professional specialist, this great amateur all-rounder is, for all his achievements and service, virtually unknown and unremembered.

George Dixon A devoted football supporter whose enthusiasm for following the fortunes of Aberdeen was undimmed, even by living on the other side of the world. From his new home in Perth, Australia, he would spare no expense in obtaining the latest news of his heroes' triumphs. For instance, on the night in 1983 that his favourite team appeared in the European Cup Winners' Cup Final, he rang his mother in Scotland and had her place the radio near the telephone so that the commentary of the entire match could be relayed to him, 12,000 miles away. The call cost him £220 but, according to Dixon, to hear Aberdeen's finest hour was worth every penny.

Bobby Dobbs (1858–1930) The fighter who boxed for so long that he ought to have got a gold watch when he retired. He started as a 17-year-old in 1875 and his professional career stretched for nearly 40 years, only ending when he reached the advanced age of 56. In between he was reckoned to have fought 1,024 bouts, very few of which were exhibitions. It was a hard way to earn a living but not as tough as it might have been, for Dobbs was an American negro and was born into slavery.

Lady Docker A wealthy socialite whose performances in the 1955 Women's World Marbles Championship excited a certain amount of controversy. She arrived at the contest in her own inimitable fashion, ensconced in the brocade seats of her gold-plated Daimler with her chauffeur Prattley at the wheel. When she stepped from this tasteless vehicle her marbling outfit was revealed – a £350 gown in peacock blue.

There were those among the 800-strong crowd at the Festival Hall in Castleford, Yorkshire who felt that this flamboyance was all gamesmanship designed to rattle the factory-girl opposition. They couldn't have known their Lady Docker. The dress was decidedly bottom-of-the-wardrobe for her and the car was the most ordinary one she owned. She could, for instance, have rolled up in the blue metallic job with the lizard skin seats or the two-seater upholstered in red crocodile or even her latest acquisition – a cream and gold item in aid of whose seat coverings six zebras had laid down their lives. No, what Yorkshire was seeing was virtually Lady Docker incognito.

Once inside the hall her ladyship put on a different kind of show. Even though she was a complete beginner at marbles she proceeded to win game after game until she was proclaimed the new champion. The marbles fraternity were horrified. They rather prided themselves on their sport's subtleties and the thought of this novice casually winning the title in between social engagements was too much for them. Mr George Burbridge, secretary of the British Marbles Board of Control, was beside himself. 'Lady Docker knows nothing about marbles and never will,' he declared and then went on to accuse her of 'trying to mock an ancient sport.' Her ladyship could take a hint. She never defended her title and soon reverted to the activity at which she was undisputed world champion: spending her husband's money.

Stephen Dockery A 19-year-old apprentice airframe fitter from Stockport who spent a ludicrous weekend in June 1982 doing nothing but winning long-distance swimming races. On the Saturday he won the nine mile Morecambe Cross-Bay race for the third successive year. Then he went to Chasewater in Staffordshire where for breakfast on Sunday he won the five mile race, had a nap, then for lunch came third in the three mile event and for tea won a one mile sprint by 20 seconds.

Charlotte Dod (1871–1960) This unassuming Cheshire girl became the most complete female sporting talent that Britain has ever produced. She won Wimbledon in 1887 when she was only 15 years old, took the title again the following year and then disappeared off on a lengthy cruise. She returned two years later to win three more championships in succession and retired undefeated at the age of 22. She then turned her attention to golf, won the British Ladies' Championship in 1904, was captain of the England hockey team, won a silver medal for archery at the 1908 Olympic Games, was a champion skater and won titles at skiing and billiards. Neither did she neglect the social graces, being an accomplished bridge player and musician.

Mrs Hessie Donahue A large and formidable American matron who once got so wild with a world heavyweight boxing champion that she knocked him out. Quite how this unlikely lady and John L. Sullivan, the 'Boston Strong Boy', found themselves together in the same ring does need a little explaining. It came about through her marriage to Charles Converse, a man who ran a school for boxers in Worcester, Massachusetts. In 1892 Converse was invited to join Sullivan in an exhibition tour of theatres. Hessie went along and, to pep up the proceedings, was asked to spar with Sullivan in a novelty item. The idea was that towards the end of the performance, when the champion had dealt with all comers, he would announce that he had been challenged by a woman.

As the crowd buzzed with this astonishing news, Hessie would step into the ring in her full prize-fighting rig-out of blouse, skirt, bloomers, long stockings and boxing gloves. She would then trade a few playful blows with Sullivan until the curtain came down. But one night this jolly tableaux got rather out of hand. Sullivan threw a punch to Hessie's face that was far harder than he intended. Riled by this departure from the script, the bruiser in bloomers let rip with a right to Sullivan's jaw and the champion dropped unconscious to the floor where he stayed for a disturbingly long time. The crowd roared its appreciation and the punch with suitable theatrical touches, was kept as part of the act.

Duke of Dorset (1745–1799) An aristocratic cricket buff. When he was envoy to France in the 1780s his missionary zeal for the game prompted him to try and introduce it into that land by organising the visit of an England touring team. But his attempt to export cricket's civilising influence was a failure. On the eve of the tour the Revolution broke out and, as the English players prepared to embark at Dover, they were amazed to see His Grace fleeing in the opposite direction. His plan remained unfulfilled.

He never really forgave the French and the old ambassador later described them in most undiplomatic language as a nation almost entirely of 'intriguing, low, artful and treacherous people'. Not, of course, that he despised all foreigners and for many years his mistress was an Italian dancer called Giovanna Francesca Antonia Guiseppe Zanerini and you can't get much more foreign than that. There is a persistent story that he dismissed this amply proportioned beauty from his favours when she ran him out during a cricket match in 1754. However, the yarn has a couple of fatal flaws: he was only nine at the time and Bacelli, as she was known, was not due in England for another 20 years.

Even without this delicious myth, his devotion to cricket was legendary enough. He played and gambled on the game with enormous gusto, maintained a 'stable' of cricketers by giving them all spurious jobs on his estate at Knole in Kent, was one of the committee that drew up the original laws of the game and, when resident in Paris, used to regularly commute by coach and ship to matches all over England. After his return from France his declining years were devoted to the patronage of art and writing. But his favourite game was never far from his thoughts and in 1797, just two years before his death, he wrote an essay which posed the rhetorical question, 'What is human life but a game of cricket?'

Fydor Dostoevsky (1821–1881) Gloomy Russian novelist whose leaden demeanour was certainly not improved by his spectacular failings as a gambler. He would bet on anything, pawning heirlooms and begging from relatives to finance his addiction. He was unfortunately a dab hand at picking non-runners, wrong numbers and poor cards and each wager only plunged him further into debt. So exciting did he find this process that he reported experiencing a sexual climax on losing at roulette. This unhappy man was a foot fetishist to boot.

J.W.H.T. Douglas (1882–1930) The only Olympic champion to captain his country at cricket. He won his gold medal at the London Games of 1908 when he beat Reginald 'Snowy' Baker for the middleweight boxing title. It was a considerable feat, for Baker was a versatile boxer who eventually won his country's championship at four different weight divisions. After the Olympics, Douglas, who was also an amateur football international, concentrated on cricket where his defensive batting style and numerous initials earnt him the nickname of 'Johnny Won't Hit Today'. He went on to captain not only England but also Essex.

Throughout his sporting life Douglas received much help and encouragement from his father. At the time of his Olympic victory Douglas Snr. was President of the Amateur Boxing Association and had the pleasure of actually handing his son his medal. Then, when Douglas was captaining Essex, his father was not only president of the club but also owned the mortgage on the county ground at Leyton. Ironically, after benefiting from all this parental aid and comfort, Douglas lost his life while trying to save the old man. They were travelling on the *SS Oberoon*, it collided with another boat off the Danish coast in 1930, Douglas Snr went overboard and his son drowned in a rescue attempt.

Mrs Billy Dovey An American housewife who developed the habit of going for lengthy cycle rides between her morning and evening household chores. In 1938 she got rather carried away with herself and covered the alarming distance of 29,604 miles – an average of 81 miles for every day of that year.

Sir Arthur Conan Doyle (1859–1930) The author and creator of Sherlock Holmes had a sporting career that was as far fetched as any of his stories. Not only was he a county footballer, excellent cricketer and international racing driver but he also turned up in some highly unlikely situations. At Lord's in 1900 he took his sole wicket in first class cricket, that of the legendary W.G. Grace; eight years later he featured in one of the most dramatic moments in Olympics history when he was one of the Games officials who assisted Italian runner Dorando Pietri in his heroic, but ultimately illegal, finish to the marathon; in 1910 he was invited to referee the World Heavyweight Championship bout between James J. Jeffries and Jack Johnson and in 1929, at the age of 70, he was to be found hurtling round the Brooklands track at over 70 mph.

Concentrating on just one pursuit was quite clearly alien to Conan Doyle's whole nature. He once said, 'I have never specialised and have therefore been a second rater in all things.' The compensation was that there was an awful lot of things at which he was 'second rate': amateur boxing, football (he played for

All-rounder and believer in fairies

Hampshire and carried on at the game until well into his forties), billiards (he once reached the third round of the Amateur Championship), skiing (he went on several gruelling cross-country expeditions and tried to teach Jerome K. Jerome), shooting (he set up Britain's first civilian rifle range and served as President of the British Field Sports Association) and motor racing (he was a member of the victorious British team in the 1911 Prince Henry Tour race).

Conan Doyle was also an intrepid cricketer. He played for the MCC against several counties, scored a century in his first match at Lord's and was a steady and reliable bowler who twice took ten wickets in an innings. Even at the age of 45 he was spritely enough to take seven Cambridgeshire wickets for 51 runs at Lord's and he was still playing for his village in Surrey at an advanced age. But Conan Doyle retained his boyish enthusiasm throughout and when he took the treasured wicket of Grace he was so overjoyed that he promptly composed a 19 stanza epic poem to celebrate the feat.

This effusive piece of verse, written when he was 41, was one of the first signs that although he may have found his touch at cricket, he was beginning to lose contact with his marbles. Soon he was taking a course in body-building from the self-styled 'Strongest Man in the World' Eugene Sandow, declaring bare-knuckle prize-fighting to be 'an excellent thing from a national point of view' and demanding that all left arm bowlers be banned from cricket by law.

These views, however, were entirely conventional when compared to the opinion he formed in 1922 about what lives at the bottom of most people's gardens. Basing his conclusions on some photographs taken by two young Yorkshire girls allegedly showing elves, gnomes and other assorted woodland folk, he wrote a book called, 'The Coming of the Fairies'. But then, after leading such a charmed sporting life, if anyone was entitled to believe in fairies it was Conan Doyle. He finally died at his Sussex home on 7 July 1930.

Six days later he was back on again. Nearly 12,000 believers were lured to a spiritualist rally at the Albert Hall by the promise of an ethereal appearance by the old scribbler. No sooner had they taken their seats than the medium, Mrs Estelle Roberts, exclaimed, 'He's here!' Alas he was gone before any great truths could be prised from him. But it was typical of a sports nut, not only game to the end but also way beyond.

Jamie Duff This Edinburgh lunatic discovered an interesting loophole in the rules of racing at Leith in the eighteenth century. Finding that there was nothing to stipulate that a horse should have four legs and a tail, he entered himself and ran the course bent at the waist in the pose of a jockey and whipped himself in with a stick. He came last.

Fred Dummett The most fragile jockey in the history of the Turf. No matter what bone he broke in his body, this Australian always came back for more punishment. In a 27 year career of riding and falling off horses he fractured his right thigh in three places, broke his foot, leg, wrist and every one of his ribs, had his right cartilage removed and broke his collar-bone 29 times.

Lord Dunblain The original Lord-a-leaping. In 1683 he was challenged to cover 60 yards in 20 jumps for a wager of 20 guineas. With his retinue of followers he went down to St James's Park, marked out a course alongside Pall Mall, flexed his exceptionally supple legs and before a vast crowd, accomplished the task with ease.

E

Wyatt Earp (1848–1928) The legendary lawman from Dodge City, he once brought a touch of the Wild West to the boxing ring. Earp was an enthusiast of the sport and was asked to referee a bout between Cornishman Bob Fitzsimmons and Tom Sharkey at San Francisco's National Athletic Club on 2 December 1896. The fight may have been held under the auspices of the Queensbury Rules but the old gunslinger was taking no chances. He entered the ring with a pair of six guns on his hips and a trigger finger ready for action.

He didn't have to wait long before using it. After only a few rounds he disqualified Fitzsimmons who then rushed forward to protest. Earp, showing the kind of form that had earned him a quick knock-out victory at the OK Corral, drew his revolver, ordered the Englishman back to his corner and then turned his gun on the angry crowd. They had begun to guess what Earp had known all along – that the fight was a fix for Sharkey.

Walter Edgerton An American boxer, known for some reason as the 'Kentucky Rosebud'. When he fought and knocked out John Henry Johnson in four rounds on 4 February 1916 he beat a man of 45 years of age. Some would say that he was merely taking an advantage of an elderly fighter. They would be wrong, for Edgerton himself was 65 and is, as far as we know, the only old age pensioner ever to fight as a professional.

King Edward VII (1841–1910) This portly monarch was apparently unable to tell the difference between a pheasant and a peasant. During a shoot at Six Mile Bottom he mistook the movements in the undergrowth of a beater for those

WYATT EARP

Boxing official and gunslinger

of a game bird, took aim, fired and shot off the poor man's kneecap. When the distinctly unornithological oaths and curses coming from the foliage revealed his mistake, the King was suitably contrite and graciously paid the beater regular compensation for the rest of his life.

Humphrey Ellis One of the last of a magnificent breed who believed that only cads and bounders played sport for cups and records. The English golf international showed his contempt for pot-hunting one glorious afternoon at Rye in Sussex. He had played wonderfully well throughout the round and he was about to chip to the final green when his caddie interrupted him. The faithful servant explained that he had totted up his master's score and thought he would wish to know that he only needed to get down in two to break the course record. The golfer looked up. 'Is that so?' he said, 'then give me my brassie (three wood).' Taking the club, Ellis then turned round and swiped the ball back towards the tee. 'That to your record,' he snorted and set off down the fairway.

M. Eshbach A French author whose *Ode To Sport* won the Olympic gold medal for literature in the art contest at the 1912 Stockholm Games. He also entered under the pseudonym of 'Georg Hohrad' but neither this nor 'M. Eschbach' was his real name. He was in fact none other than Baron de Coubertin, the founder of the modern Olympic movement.

Joe Ezar The trick shot golfer who played a round in a million. The year was 1936, the event was the Italian Open and the scene was the Sestriere Golf Club. Ezar had finished his third round and was giving the gallery an exhibition of novelty strokes when up stepped the President of the Fiat Motor Company. He had watched the display with growing amazement and remarked that if Ezar could predict his shots with such precision, then he could well break the course record of 67 the next day. The president offered him 5,000 lire if he did so. 'How much for a 64?' Ezar asked casually. 'Forty thousand lire', came the reply.

As he stood there, the idea of having a go at such an absurdly low score began to appeal to him. He asked for a cigarette packet and in front of the crowd wrote down a hole-by-hole score for a 64. It was no more than the gesture of a showman. The odds against achieving this detailed forecast were reckoned to be several million to one and by the following morning the cigarette pack prediction was being dismissed as a harmless prank. Even when his score over the opening holes matched his nominated totals, no one took much notice. But as hole succeeded hole and Ezar kept pace with his fantasy scorecard, the gallery started to hum with excitement. Suddenly, they and the golfing hustler realised that his light-hearted forecast might actually come true.

And so it might have done if it had not been for the ninth hole. The cigarette packet said an eagle three there, yet he was still 50 yards short of the green after his second shot. He only managed a birdie four but he immediately responded with a three at the next, instead of the four he had nominated, to keep his overall score bang on course. He nonchalantly played out the rest of the round exactly as he said he would, returned a 64 and duly collected his money from the astonished President of Fiat.

F

J. N. Farrar When most golfers talk about a handicap they mean a number from one to 28. Mr Farrar, however, thought the words should be taken more literally. So when he stepped onto Royston golf course one afternoon in 1914, he was dressed in full infantry marching order, complete with water bottle, rifle, full field kit and haversack. He had struck a bet that he could go round in under 100 shots in spite of his cumbersome load. He made it with a 94 and went off to war secure in the knowledge that if it came to an 18 hole play-off with the Germans, he would be ready for them.

J. Smith Ferebee In 1938 this American amateur golfer won more money from the game in four days than Ben Hogan, Sam Snead and other top professionals did all year. He did it by winning a bet that he could not play 600 holes of golf in just four days. Apart from having to average over eight full rounds a day, there were additional complications. The courses chosen were in eight cities spread right across America and Ferebee had to break 90 in each of the 33⅓ rounds he played. But the Chicago broker calculated that the stake of $150,000 and the right to a plantation worth $30,000 was well worth the risk of failure. He decided to take on the challenge.

Starting in Los Angeles, where he played 84 holes, he flew on to Phoenix, Arizona (81 holes, 36 of them after 9 p.m.), Kansas City (72 holes), St Louis (72 holes), Milwaukee (72 holes), Chicago (75 holes), Philadelphia (72 holes) and finally New York (72 holes). He employed 110 caddies, used torches and flares at night and the only rest he ever had was when he was on the plane flying between courses.

Joseph Fillison (1862–1964) A former professional slow bowler who umpired for the BBC Cricket Club at the age of 100. He must have made something of an impression because a few months later he was officiating at Lord's for an Old England v Lord's Taverners match. Only in cricket could a job which requires acute hearing and twenty-twenty vision be given to a man of such advanced years.

Ivor Finn One of the most aptly named human beings in the history of the universe. He was chairman of the Leicester Swimming Club in the 1960s.

Maurice Flitcroft This Barrow-in-Furness crane driver very much wanted to play in the British Open Golf Championship. The fact that he had never played the game in his life, had no clubs and thought a bunker was something that you put the coal in, was neither here nor there. He had seen the event on television and was determined to walk the fairways in the company of Jack Nicklaus and the game's other stars. So in 1976 he ordered a set of clubs from a mail order catalogue, sent in his entry to St Andrews as a professional and began practising in the fields behind his house. A few months later the 46-year-old set off for Formby for the pre-qualifying round of the Open Championship.

As he stepped onto the first tee his playing partners had no way of knowing what an extraordinary golfer Flitcroft was. They soon found out. From the moment he unveiled his unorthodox swing to the time when he mercifully holed out at the 18th, they watched in open-mouthed amazement. He zig-zagged from tee to green, hacked at the ball in the rough and putted like a man determined to avoid the hole. His grasp of the game's rules and etiquette seemed only tenuous at best and the witnesses to his memorable performance were agreed on one thing: they had never seen a golfer quite like Maurice Flitcroft.

When all the fluffs, slices, hooks, tops, skiers, shanks, sockets and air shots had been counted up, the score that was put beside the name of Maurice Flitcroft (Unattached) was 121. It was, by a good few dozen, the highest ever recorded in the Open. On the other hand, one had to remember, and who could really forget it, that it was the crane driver's first ever full round of golf.

As is the practice among golf professionals who have just shot a sensational score, he then gave an audience to the waiting press. 'I felt the pressure of the big event,' he told them, 'I wasn't really ready for this championship. To be frank I was a bit erratic, but I started to put it together towards the end of the round.' (Presumably a reference to his only par of the day at the 14th.) 'I am completely self-taught you know but then I've always been a bit of an athlete. I thought it would be nice to play in the Open with Jack Nicklaus and that lot, it would give me some encouragement. After all, I haven't reached my peak yet, some of those top stars have been at it for years. They are well past their best. I am going to improve and be back next year and then watch out!'

The ones who were watching out were the Open's organisers, the Royal and Ancient. When his entry duly came in they said they were now empowered to demand evidence of ability. Flitcroft's plea that he had improved considerably and was prepared to stage a demonstration of his skills around the Old Course at St Andrews did not impress them. They rejected his entry and were confident that they had seen the last of Maurice at the Open. That's what they thought. On three other occasions in the next few years he entered the Open under an alias, made a cricket score over the first nine holes in the qualifying round and withdrew before he was unmasked.

So, little did they suspect in 1983 that the entry from 53-year-old Gerald Hoppy of Switzerland was from none other than their old friend the Barrow-in-Furness crane driver. No one recognised him when he showed up on the first tee at Pleasington for the pre-qualifying round, no alarm bells rang as he lurched into his opening drive and none of his partners guessed his true identity when he scored six at the first hole. But when he took five putts from eight feet at the second to run up a nine, followed that with an eight at the 3rd and a 10 at the 6th, the penny began to drop. As his ball fell into the hole for an eight at the ninth and an outward score of 63, an official of the Royal and Ancient tapped him on the shoulder.

After a brief conversation, Monsieur Hoppy, alias Maurice Flitcroft, withdrew. He was very disappointed and he told reporters, 'I expected to do a little better but my practice yesterday was interrupted by a terrible headache.' However bad it was, it could not have been anything to the headaches he had caused the Royal and Ancient Golf Club by his unusual appearances at their championship.

Leo Flynn A member of the Jack Dempsey entourage and a highly original cheat on the golf course. He took up the game late in life, became obsessed with it and was soon playing to a single figure handicap. It was remarkable progress, made all the more swift by his almost total disregard for the rules. At first it was an improved lie here, an altered score there but in time he graduated to more elaborate arrangements. His most inspired stroke was to engage the services of a negro caddie who always walked the course barefoot. Whenever Flynn's ball went into the rough it was the duty of this loyal factotum to pick it up with his unusually long and prehensile toes and, without stooping, deposit it silently down on the fairway. He accomplished this while affecting an air of preoccupied innocence which his master then matched with a show of delighted amazement at finding his ball sitting up perfectly on the short grass.

Gerald Ford Former President of the United States and homicidal golfer. In pro-am and pro-celebrity events the world over he was notorious for hitting members of the gallery from even the most unlikely lies. His secret service staff, who on the pretext of working under-cover hid themselves behind trees and in bushes, suffered lighter casualties. Comedian Bob Hope used to say that when Ford golfed at Pinehurst, where there are several courses, the old President never knew precisely which one he would be playing until after he had teed off.

In his youth, however, he had been a brilliant gridiron footballer. His play as centre at Michigan between 1931 and 1935 was so impressive that both the Chicago Bears and Detroit Lions made him offers to turn professional. He rejected them, coached football and boxing at Yale and then went into politics.

Malcolm W. Ford This American athlete won three national titles at 100 yards, two at 200 yards, one at the high jump, five at the long jump, was the US all-round athletics champion three times, won the Amateur Athletics Association long jump title, set a world record for the long jump, was a successful Boston lawyer and a dollar millionaire. Life, however, lacked a certain something. On 8 May 1902 in New York City he shot and killed his brother Paul, then turned the gun on himself and committed suicide.

Gerald Forsberg It was July 1983. The time was mid-afternoon and the scene was a Devon beach at the start of a long-distance swimming race. The competitors came to the line, a small round figure in his 70s fired the starting gun and the swimmers were off. So too was the starter. For as soon as the race was under way the old age pensioner handed his gun, flat hat and raincoat to a bystander, dashed into the surf and struck out for Fishcombe Cove, Brixham, four miles away.

What might have appeared to onlookers as a wanton act of self-destruction was in fact routine behaviour for Gerald Forsberg, OBE, RN Commander (retd) and almost certainly the oldest ocean-going swimmer in the world. After all, he had that year already swum the four miles around Grimsby Docks during a violent hail and thunder storm, raced the three mile length of Lake Bala in North Wales while 30 other swimmers dropped out and swum several other gruelling races.

His long distance career began in 1949 when some naval cadets entered him for the Ryde to Southsea race as a practical joke. Very soon it was Forsberg who was laughing, for he took to the sport like a natural. He went on to hold the record for the English Channel, Bristol Channel, Morecambe Bay two-way, Lake Windermere two-way and Lough Neagh. By the time he was 70 years old Forsberg had swum well over 9,000 miles in competition and training, a distance he preferred to express as the nautical distance from London to Singapore. He won the Observer Sports Nut of the Year award in 1982.

William 'Fatty' Foulke (1874–1916) The most imposing obstacle to goal-scorers ever to step onto a football field. As a goalkeeper he had one impeccable credential – he filled more of the space between the posts than any man before or since. He stood 6 foot 2½ inches in height and towards the end of his career weighed in at 26 stone. Even in his younger days with Sheffield United and England, he tipped the scales at anything up to 19 stone and by the time he appeared in the 1902 FA Cup Final against Southampton, his weight was 21 stone and rising.

Of course, in the goalkeeping sense, Foulke rose less and less as the years went by. But when he did, it was an awesome sight. With a great thrust of his legs he would somehow overcome the gravitational pull of his huge bulk and leave his goal-mouth launch-pad with all moving parts in motion, some in different directions. Once airborne, his body would settle on a general trajectory until he returned shudderingly to earth, where the area of impact would be marked by a small crater.

As can be imagined, he was not a man to be trifled with. Forwards who charged him were quite likely to be seized round the waist and hurled by Foulke into the net and in 1894 he found Liverpool forward George Allen so annoyingly persistent that he picked him up by the ankles and bounced him up and down on his head in the goalmouth.

However, he reserved the full force of his majestic temper for referees. At the end of the 1902 Cup Final he left the field huffing and puffing with indignation at a decision by Mr Tom Kirkham which allowed Southampton to equalize and earn a replay. In the dressing room Foulke got more and more worked up so that by the time he was stripped, his entire mass was wobbling with rage. With a great roar Foulke swore vengeance on the little official and went looking for him. Fortunately Kirkham saw him first and he dived for cover into a nearby boot cupboard. But Foulke was not to be thwarted. He seized the cupboard door and began trying to wrench it from its hinges. It was in this rather compromising position that the naked goalkeeper was then discovered by the Secretary of the Football Association and several other worthies. They somehow managed to soothe the savage Foulke and shepherd him gently back to his dressing room.

Three years later he was transferred to Chelsea where his season with them was distinguished as much for his eating as his playing. Once, on an away trip, he declined to join his team-mates on an early morning training walk. When they returned they found Foulke asleep under the dining room table, having demolished all eleven breakfasts. As they began to harangue him, he replied, 'I don't care what you call me, as long as you don't call me late for dinner.'

He saw out his playing days with Bradford City and then fell upon harder and harder times. By 1916 the man who had appeared in three Cup Finals was reduced to a sideshow freak, earning pennies by saving penalties from holiday-makers on Blackpool Sands. One day in May he caught pneumonia from his exertions on the chilly beach and within a few days he was dead, aged only 41.

Frederick Louis, Prince of Wales (d. 1751) The eldest son of George II and a devoted cricket nut. He was Surrey's first recorded captain and always enjoyed spicing up the interest of a flagging game with a modest wager. With the Earl of Middlesex he once organised a match on horseback at Bromley for a stake of £1,000. Despite the problem of having four legs with which to be lbw. Middlesex's mounted batsmen scored 72 before the Prince's side replied with a magnificent 95 equestrian runs.

Cricket, however, was his undoing. In 1751 this spirited heir to the throne was hit on the side by a cricket ball. He never recovered, dying from his injuries at his Cliveden home just a few weeks later. Thus did the national game deprive the country of its first King Fred. It was not the first, or the last, time that sport was to interfere with a royal succession. France, never a nation that took great care with its monarchs, had Kings Louis X and Charles VIII die from the effects of real tennis and in this century King Albert I of the Belgians was killed while engaged in the more obviously dicey pursuit of mountaineering.

Otto Froitzheim A German tennis player whose experiences at Wimbledon gave him a somewhat inflated idea of the influence wielded by the championship organisers, the All England Lawn Tennis Croquet Club. He had finished as runner-up in the all-comers' round of the men's singles in 1914, losing to the future champion Norman Brookes of Australia. Yet within a few months tennis was the least of his problems. The First World War broke out and, swelled with Teutonic pride, he enlisted in the Kaiser's Army. Visions of military glory wafted before his eyes. Would he soon be adding the Iron Cross to all his tennis trophies? No. Shortly after going off to the front in his brand new spiked helmet he was taken prisoner by the British.

Froitzheim was devastated. He thought it monstrous that he should have to spend the rest of the war incarcerated in this fashion. So he sat down and wrote a letter, probably the most curious one ever received at Wimbledon. It was to George Hillyard, the Secretary of the All England Club, and asked him to use his influence to have Froitzheim freed. He pleaded that it was unsporting to keep him from fighting for Germany. The British authorities, however, thought that this was stretching their famed sense of fair play a bit too far and they rejected the request.

Charles Burgess Fry (1872–1956) One of sport's immortal all-rounders. He was a triple blue at Oxford where he naturally obtained a first, held the world long jump record for 21 years, represented England at soccer, appeared in the 1902 FA Cup Final, played rugby for Blackheath and the Barbarians and was one of the greatest cricketers of all time. He scored 30,886 runs for England, Oxford University, Surrey, Sussex and Hampshire, played in 26 Test matches, six of them as captain, hit 94 centuries and once scored six hundreds in successive innings.

Although he was sufficiently prized in his own land to be offered the England cricket captaincy at the age of 49, the esteem in which he was held on the Continent of Europe knew almost no bounds. While he was working at the League of Nations an Albanian bishop approached him in all seriousness with a formal request to become king of that country and Adolf Hitler sought his advice before setting up the Nazi Youth movement. To his eternal credit, Fry declined both invitations.

G

K.G. Gandar Dower (1908–1944) During the late 1930s this poet and explorer conducted one of the most absurd sporting experiments ever recorded. For some reason he got it into his head that there was something amiss with greyhound racing. His solution was simple: replace the dogs with cheetahs. So in 1937 he imported a team of eight animals from the jungles of Kenya and introduced them onto London's dog tracks.

The only trouble was that the fastest mammal on earth turned out to be a bit of a bad sport. In a head to head race at Romford Stadium it was found that as soon as one cheetah edged ahead, the other would stop running and refuse to finish the course. Further trials at Harringay a few months later proved that *Acononyx jubatus* was also not prepared to shift out of second gear in these artificial surroundings. With the scent of fresh gazelle wafting up his nostrils, the cheetah had been known to get up to 60–63 mph across the savannah but the sight of a tin-plate hare jerking round a dog track inspired it to no more than 43 mph.

This speed still meant that a cheetah could give a greyhound 20 yards start over 345 yards and beat it, but it was a good deal less than full cry and the punters were unimpressed. Much to the relief of the nation's dog breeders the project was abandoned.

The sporting world then settled back to see what other little innovations Gandar Dower had up his sleeve. After all he had plenty of experience to draw on, having played cricket for Harrow, represented Cambridge University at tennis, rugby fives, Eton fives, real tennis, squash and billiards, won national titles at three of these sports and played tennis for Great Britain. Sadly, no one ever found out what else he had in mind. The war came and towards the end of it, in February 1944, he was lost at sea.

John Warne Gates Legendary American gambler who would bet on anything – horses, baseball, even on which raindrop would slide down a windowpane first. In fact he had such a good eye for the pedigree of a water droplet that he once won $20,000 on a train journey through a rainstorm.

The funds for this incessant wagering came from his barbed wire business which by the 1890s he had built up into the largest company in the industry. Thus he could afford to win and lose huge bets with stylish nonchalance. He was said to have lost $375,000 in one afternoon on the racetrack but on another occasion to have won over $600,000 on one of his own horses. Gambling on such a heroic scale as this certainly scared the hell out of the bookies and at one meeting the inevitable happened: he was asked to limit his bets to $10,000. Gates was so outraged that he defiantly offered to put $1,000,000 on one horse. There were no takers but the incident gave him his nickname, 'Bet-A-Million' Gates.

Just after his fiftieth birthday this outlandish character began to drift away from the racetracks and by 1909 he was to be found warning of the evils of gambling at a church conference. The word was that he had renounced betting and got religion but knowing Gates he probably had a few dollars with the preacher on how many converts they would get.

George VI (1895–1952) The bowler who took the most remarkable hat-trick in the history of cricket. In a family match on the slopes below Windsor Castle he dismissed three successive Kings of England with three consecutive deliveries. His royal flush consisted of Edward VII, George V and Edward VIII, although none of them, it must be said, could be regarded as first class in the cricketing sense. In later life George distinguished himself in more serious arenas by playing in the men's doubles at Wimbledon in 1926 with Sir Louis Grieg and captaining the Royal and Ancient Golf Club in 1930.

Prince George of Greece A guest of honour at the 1896 Olympics, he stepped from the stands and upstaged a gold medal winner. George had just finished watching Britain's Launceston Elliot win the single-handed weightlifting event when he saw the official responsible for removing the weights sweating and straining even to budge them. This was the opportunity he had been looking for. He was allegedly one of the strongest men in Europe but his royal birth had so far denied him the chance to prove it. Not this time however. In one bound he was out of his seat and across the track. With no trouble at all he picked up the heaviest weight that had been used in competition (156 pounds), threw it a considerable distance and accepted the cheers of the crowd.

J. Paul Getty Multi-millionaire oil tycoon and notorious skinflint whose grasping ways evidently gave his fist alarming strength. In an argument over a girl, Getty once laid out Jack Dempsey with a left uppercut. It was the only time that the 'Manassa Mauler', who held the world heavyweight boxing crown for seven years, was ever knocked out.

Tommy Gildert This 38-year-old machine minder was not content with just running from John O'Groats to Land's End, he also wanted to make the journey even tougher than it was. So to warm up at the start he casually broke three 'Super Stars' world records – 122 squat thrusts in a minute, 44 chin-ups in a minute and 98 parallel bar dips in the same time – and then set off. Leaving the northernmost tip of Britain on 1 August 1982, he ran the 840 miles to the south arriving in Land's End 20 days later. Lest anyone think that was too easy, he had incorporated 30,210 press-ups along the way.

Lord Glascow A nineteenth century racehorse owner whose strange ways were a considerable thorn in the side of the Jockey Club. The problem was that he had a deep and abiding aversion to naming his horses. Instead of calling them something like 'Shergar' or 'Red Rum' or even 'Dobbin', he would enter them as 'brother of this' or 'sister to that'. This habit caused such confusion and inconvenience to the club that eventually they brought in a rule that no horse aged three and up should run unnamed. That should fix Lord Glascow, they thought. But his devious old lordship was their equal. He complied with the letter of the new rule but not, one imagines, its spirit, christening one horse 'Give-Him-A-Name', another 'He-Doesn't-Want-A-Name' and a third 'He's-Not-Worth-A-Name'.

Apart from getting up the noses of the Jockey Club, his other ambition in life was to have one of these peculiarly named beasts win a classic. He spent a vast fortune in breeding, buying and selling thoroughbreds and hired and fired an endless succession of trainers. Neither did he spare the horses. His method of sorting out those animals which came up to scratch and eliminating those that did not was wonderfully simple. He would go to his training establishment at Middleham and summon five or six jockeys to ride a score or more trials on all his horses. The half a dozen or so animals who were least successful would then

J. PAUL GETTY

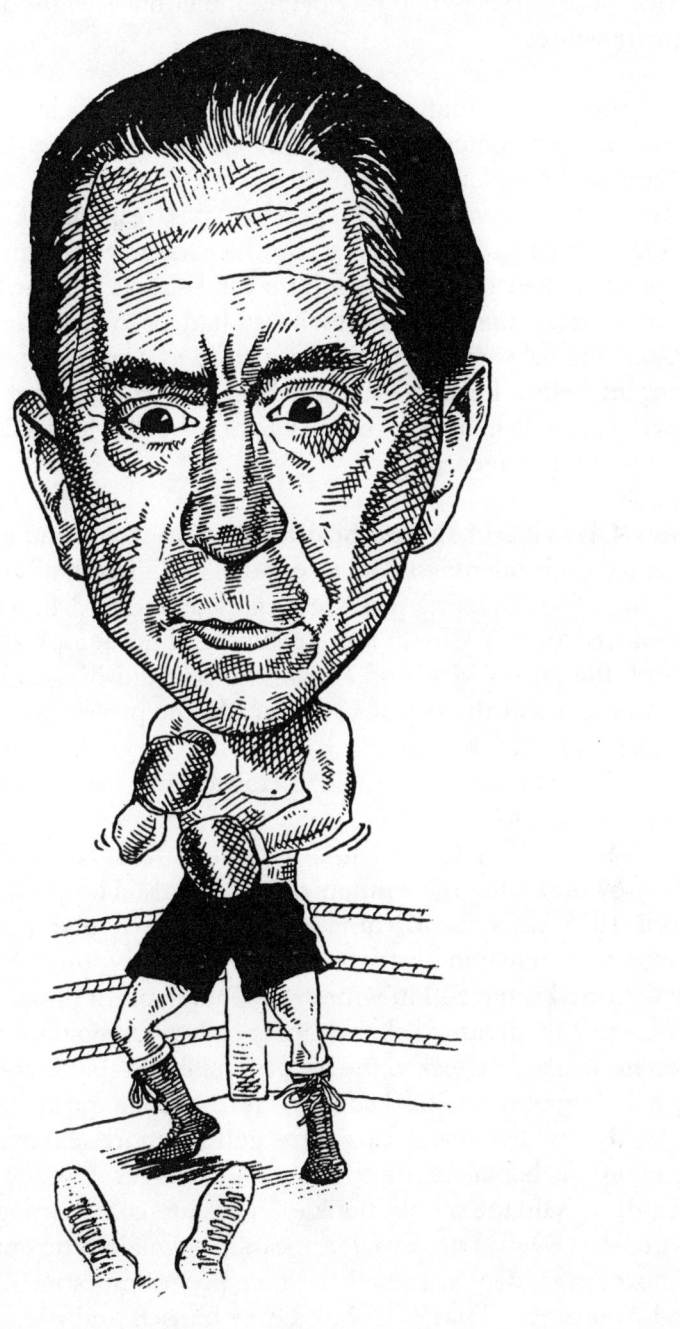

Bruiser and billionaire

be shot. Mercifully he did not apply this survival of the fittest policy to humans who ran poorly in the great race of life, and he once fed the destitute of Paisley for an entire winter.

Freddy Glaus The manager of Surinam's athletics team, he set a new Olympic record for incompetence at the 1960 Games in Rome. In theory his task as manager was simple; after all his team consisted of just one athlete, 800 metres runner Wim Essayas. But in practice this responsibility proved too great. Having arrived in Rome, Glaus and his charge rested and then the following afternoon turned up at the stadium for Essayas's event. This was a bit of a shame because the 800 metres heats had been held in the morning. Thus Essayas, the sole representative of a third of a million people, was out of the Olympics before he had even got changed. He was not, as it turned out, a forgiving man. When they got back to South America he filed a lawsuit against his forgetful manager.

Sidney Gleave and Ernest Smith A motor-cyclist and golf professional who combined their talents to play a round of golf in each of five different countries on a single day. Starting in Prestwick, Scotland at 3.40 a.m. on 12 June 1939, they moved on via Gleave's motorbike and an aeroplane, to play courses in Ireland, the Isle of Man and England before finishing in Hawarden, Wales at 8.15 p.m. To win the bet of £100, Smith, the professional at Daryhulme Golf Club, Manchester, had to break 80 in all five rounds. He did so by scoring 70, 76, 76, 72 and finally a record 68 at Hawarden.

John Godley This Oxford undergraduate fulfilled every punter's favourite fantasy by dreaming the winners of horse races. The visions began one night in March 1946 when he dreamed that two particular horses would win the following day. He told his friends, they backed the animals and when both won they collected some £40 in winnings. Godley put it down to coincidence but a month later he dreamed that a horse called Tubemoore had won at Aintree. When he awoke he checked the papers and found that there was no Tubemoore, only a Tubemoose. He backed it and it romped home at 100–6.

By July the nocturnal tips were getting more elaborate. He saw himself ringing up his bookmaker and asking him the result of the last race. 'Certainly Mr Godley,' said the spooky bookie, 'It has just come through. Monumental has won at 5-4.' (Even in dreams, it appears, bookmakers do not give good odds.) In the morning Godley searched the race programmes until he came to a horse called Mentores. 'That's it,' he said to himself and placed his bet. When he phoned his bookie and requested the result he received the reply, 'Certainly Mr Godley, it has just come through. Mentores won at 6-4.'

After this success Godley slept undisturbed for a while. Then, one Friday night in 1947, he dreamed he was at Lingfield. He saw a horse ridden by Edgar Britt win a race in the Gaekwar of Baroda's colours and then a hot favourite – possibly called The Bogey – win the next race easily. This time he was ready to go public with his strange powers. So on the Saturday he prepared a witnessed account of his dream and at 2.30 p.m. deposited it in the safe of an Oxford postmaster. At 3.45 p.m. he rang the offices of the *Daily* and *Sunday Mirror* (*Pictorial* as it was then), told them his story and gave the forecast contained in his affidavit – Baroda Squadron for the 4 p.m. at Lingfield and The Brogue for the 4.30 p.m. Both won.

The *Mirror*, suitably impressed, recovered the sworn statement from the postmaster, ran a story and offered Godley a job as a tipster. Thereafter he had mixed fortunes and gradually his dreams faded away. But suddenly in 1958, appropriately in the gamblers' Mecca of Monte Carlo, they made a brief comeback. In his sleep he saw the Grand National won by What Man, the third favourite. There was, in fact, no What Man but among the runners there was a Mr What, a 66-1 outsider. Godley kept his money in his pocket but by the day of the race when the horse had come down to 18-1 and third favourite, he could resist no longer. He backed it with £25 and duly collected £450 in winnings.

Not surprisingly, after pulling a stunt like that, the visions departed, never to return. As to an explanation for his elusive gift, Godley himself was baffled. When he reported his experiences to the Psychical Research Society they could only suggest that his selections were subconscious ones made during the day which then re-emerged in a more memorable form during the night. What is certain is that the man who saw winners in his sleep went on to become Lord Kilbracken and a distinguished foreign correspondent. Few who met him in later life as the President of British-Kurdish Friendship Society could ever have guessed that they were also meeting a man who had once worked as a tabloid's racing tipster. It was a possibility they would never have dreamed of.

Golden Beach An independent sort of racehorse that got fed up running in the 4.45 at Newton Abbot and decided to try and take a short cut home instead. One could hardly blame the animal. It was, after all, just an every day two mile hurdle at the small Devon course and any interest Golden Beach may have had in the outcome rather disappeared when its rider was unseated. So when the other runners turned into the home stretch, the seven-year-old horse didn't join them but ran straight on through a gap in the rails.

It leapt the five foot high fence that divided the course from a nearby railway and headed off along the embankment. The fugitive even galloped past a train which was pulling out of a station, much to the amazement of the driver. On it went past signals and points until, in the village of Kingskerswell four miles down the line, it finally came to a halt. Apart from a few cuts and bruises Golden Beach was none the worse for wear. But after that day in 1983 it would always be remembered as the gelding that lost its marbles.

The Golf Green Gang A bunch of sporting criminals. They admired the delicate nap of the sixth green at Addington Court Golf Club in Surrey so much that one night in the spring of 1983 they stole 12 square yards of its turf.

Harry Gonder The hole in one is the most coveted stroke of luck in sport and this golf enthusiast was determined to get one. So one day in 1940 he stepped onto the tee of a 160 yard short hole at his home course vowing not to leave it until he had claimed his prize. Beginning at 10.15 in the morning he fired shot after shot at the flag in rapid succession. Too rapid as it turned out, for by the time he broke off for food after the 941st attempt, only his 86th stroke had remotely threatened the target.

Hour after fruitless hour passed. His shots went in front of the green, over the green, right of the green, left of the green and even, in a number of celebrated cases, actually on the green; but never in the hole. He had his moments, of course, like the 996th which hit the pin and bounced out and numbers 1,162 and 1,184 which landed mere inches from the cup. But midnight and shot 1,600 came and went unrewarded. By now his hands were blistering badly yet this handicap, his fatigue and the deepening darkness seemed somehow to improve his aim. Number 1,750 hit the hole and came out and a few minutes later 1,756 did the same.

Encouraged by these near misses, the resolute little figure dug into his reserves and at 2.40 a.m. he found the strength for just one more shot. As it soared away towards the green he felt a thrill of excitement. Would this at last be his hole in one? No. With a disappointing thud it landed ten feet from the pin. Gonder knew when he was beaten. Sixteen hours 25 minutes and 1,817 strokes earlier he had been convinced that one only had to stand there and play enough shots at the hole for it to yield up an ace. Now he knew better. As he picked up his things and trudged back to the clubhouse, he was certain that the law of averages was an ass.

Joey Goodchild This football supporter's engaging performances as a tap dancer enlivened many a half-time at Watford during the 1920s. What made them particularly praiseworthy was that they took place on the roof of the main stand. But although the acoustics of this structure were admirable for his purposes, its height was not and one day the inevitable happened. After accomplishing a breathtaking glissando which climaxed on the very edge of the guttering, Joey lost his balance and fell towards the crowd below. Spinning through the air with as much grace as he could muster, the old dancer ricocheted off a gentleman, broke his glasses and came to rest on a lady, who was understandably rather put out. So were Watford. The club had to apologise to the gentleman and pay the lady £25 compensation. Not unreasonably they told Joey that his dancing years were over.

Thomas Gisborne Gordon A one-handed rugby international. He had lost his right hand in a childhood shooting accident but the lack of it did not prevent him winning three caps for Ireland at wing-threequarter in 1877 and 1878. He was on the losing side each time.

Vere Thomas St Leger Gould (1854–1909) The only Wimbledon finalist, so far, to have been convicted for murder. A baronet's son, he overcame the handicap of having a name like a pedigree dog's and by his twenties was a brilliant tennis player. In 1879 he won the Irish championship and went on to reach the final of the men's singles at Wimbledon that year where he lost to the Revd J. T. Hartley 6-2, 6-4, 6-2.

The experience of losing to a clergyman may have helped convince him that life's line calls were going against him for, shortly after retiring from tennis, he began to harbour some very anti-social thoughts indeed. These culminated in 1907 when he and his French wife Violet murdered Emma Levin, a wealthy Dutch widow. The deed was done in Monte Carlo and they dismembered the body and tried to ship the various bits and pieces back to England in a pair of trunks. The gruesome luggage was intercepted in transit and its discovery led to the swift arrest and conviction of Gould and his wife. She was packed off to chokey in France and he was sent to the Devil's Island penal colony where he died 18 months later.

Dr E.M. Grace A resourceful cricketer who on 15 August 1877 employed a broomstick to score a century against a Cheltenham XI. Besides being a dab hand with the household implements, he was also the brother of the great WG and, in what time he could spare away from the cricket field, the coroner at Thornbury in Gloucestershire. He was, however, always careful that these mere matters of life and death did not intrude too much on his sport. Once, when he was playing at some far-flung county ground, a reply-paid telegram arrived summoning him home for an inquest. Acting on the instructions of his brother, the absentee coroner wired back, 'Impossible to come today. Please put corpse on ice.'

Like his fabled relative, EM's enthusiasm for the fray sometimes prompted him to take certain liberties with the laws of the game. On one occasion, when bowling for Thornbury, he saw the last four balls of his over hit for six by a Weston-Super-Mare batsman called F. A. Leeston-Smith. 'Over,' called the umpire. 'The devil it is,' said the intimidating old Grace, 'I'm going to have another one.' He did and the bemused batsman was stumped. It was one of many destructive performances that he gave for his village side. Even in his last season for them, at the age of 68, he was still spry enough to take 119 wickets.

W.G. Grace (1848–1915) Victorian sporting legend and the most famous cricketer who ever lived. He was regarded with such reverence throughout the English-speaking world that when he died of natural causes in London on 23 October 1915, the Germans tried to boost their flagging morale by claiming him as an air-raid victim.

He may have made his reputation at cricket – scoring 53,856 runs and taking 2,763 wickets – but he also earned distinction in other areas. In 1866, after having scored 224 for All England against Surrey at the Oval, he absented himself from the field, nipped down to Crystal Palace and won the 440 yards hurdles at the National Olympian Association's championships. The amazing Grace was also skilled at curling, billiards, golf and bowls, captaining England in their first international against Scotland in 1903. He received countless honours, none more curious than the medal awarded him in 1895 by the Balloon Society of Great Britain for 'promoting the healthy development and preservation of the characteristics of active Englishmen.'

Donald Grant An energetic golfer. In 1939 he cycled the 600 miles from London to Dornoch in the highlands of Scotland, competed in the open amateur tournament, finished second and pedalled all the way back again.

Clifford Gray (1892–1941) The most unassuming gold medallist in Olympic history. He won two golds with the United States four man bobsleigh team at the Winter Games of 1928 and 1932 yet he was so modest that his children did not know of his achievements until after he died. They, and the rest of the world, knew him better for the songs he composed, which included 'Got a date with an angel' and 'If you were the only girl in the world'.

Harry Greb (1894–1926) A world boxing champion who, unknown to all but himself, defended his title several times while blind in one eye. His handicap was only revealed when he died following an eye operation two months after losing the middleweight crown to Tiger Flowers. Until he entered hospital Greb was thought to be almost indestructible. Known as 'The Human Windmill' because his arms seemed to be in perpetual motion, he was the only man ever to defeat the great Gene Tunney, held his world title for three years, made nine defences of it, won over 300 bouts and was only knocked out once, when he was 20 and only then because he had sustained a broken arm.

Greenwich Pensioners This company of adventurous old soldiers staged a cricket match in 1796 that went clean over the boundaries of good taste. They formed a team of one-legged veterans and played a match at Walworth against eleven men with only one arm. This highly competitive fixture was not without its attendant risks and there were five broken legs – mercifully wooden ones. Those lacking a lower limb, presumably bowling long hops, eventually triumphed by the distressingly symbolic margin of 111 runs.

Hon. Robert Grimstone (1816–1884) Since time immemorial cricketers have found life simpler if they took only one bat at a time to the wicket. Grimstone was the exception, he took two. One was of regular size and the other was for when he knew he might have to face Alfred Mynn, the most feared bowler of the day. This implement weighed 3lbs and was two inches longer in the shoulder and two inches shorter in the handle than conventional bats. So effectively did it do its work that he called it 'Mynn's Master'.

In later life, however, he was averse to change of all kinds and this temperament qualified him admirably for the Presidency of the MCC. In conservative circles his term of office is still celebrated for his stubborn refusal to introduce mowing machines at Lord's; a decision which, if nothing else, gave a stay of execution to the ground's flock of loyal sheep.

Grove Cricket Club (circa 1930) Visitors to this Berkshire club often used to wonder why its pavilion looked like a horse box. There was a simple answer, it *was* a horse box, the very one in which Humourist, the 1921 Derby winner, had travelled to Epsom.

H

George Hackenschmidt (1877–1968) Russian physical fitness freak who at the age of 85 was able to do 50 consecutive jumps over the back of a chair. This obsession with strenuous and apparently meaningless exercise had begun in his teens when he gave a milkman's horse the shock of its life by lifting it onto his shoulders and carrying it about. He then went on to win world and national titles at wrestling and weightlifting. But he was never the conventional idea of a muscle man. In middle age he turned to philosophy and wrote books, including the splendidly titled *Man and Cosmic Antagonism to Mind and Spirit*. He was, perhaps, the world's first existentialist strongman and certainly was one of the few who could pronounce that phrase.

Oliver Halassy (1904–1946) When young Oliver was run over by a tram at the age of 11 and had his left leg cut off just below the knee, a career in international sport seemed rather out of the question. But this Hungarian survived the trauma and went on to become one of the greatest water polo players of all time. He was capped 96 times and between 1927 and 1936 helped his country to win two gold medals and one silver at the Olympics and a pair of European titles. As a solo swimmer, one and a half of his legs were often better than two of anyone else's and he had 25 national records and the European 1500 metres Freestyle Championship of 1931 to prove it. He died aged only 37 when he was shot dead as he returned home one night.

Sir Edward Marshall Hall QC (1858–1929) A barrister and boxing enthusiast. His win on points in one of the most important sporting trials of the century saved boxing for future generations. The case was one of manslaughter and followed the death of one Murray Livingstone. Fighting under the name of Billy Smith, he had fallen and hit his head on a corner post in a bout with Jack Roberts at the National Sporting Club on 4 April 1901. Roberts and nine members of the club were then committed to the Old Bailey for 'feloniously killing and slaying Livingstone' which, even in the language of the day, was putting it a bit strong.

Nevertheless the trial, with Sir Edward defending Roberts, was something of a test case. If there was an acquittal then boxers could go on climbing into the ring knowing that whatever unpleasantness took place they were free from judicial reprisals. But if the verdict went against the defendants, anyone involved with a boxing match in which a fighter died could expect to face criminal charges and a possible prison sentence.

Boxing itself was on trial. In the blue corner was the argument that although death was not exactly an inevitable consequence of a boxing bout, it was sufficiently heard of for there to be criminal negligence involved in staging such a dangerous spectacle. In the red corner was the manly pursuits theory, championed, with almost excessive vigour, by an array of defending counsel. Chief among these was Sir Edward, never an advocate who believed in an understated performance. As he stood in court, robes puffed up with righteous indignation, he threw everything he had at the prosecution. Referring to their 'misdirected zeal for public safety', he defended boxing to the hilt and his speech climaxed with perhaps the most sustained piece of sarcasm ever heard in a court of law.

'I suggest,' he began, 'that in all future boxing competitions, whether held at the National Sporting Club or anywhere else, the combatants should wear leather jerkins, under which bells should be concealed – electric, if possible. The boxing gloves should be of the largest size and should be plentifully smeared with chalk. For each chalk mark seen on the opponent's doublet the striker should be given a point. But if in the making of that mark he should happen to ring one of the bells, he should be instantly disqualified for unnecessary violence with the intention of effecting a knock-out and be rendered liable to an indictment for manslaughter.'

Swayed by this one-two from the big-wig, the jury returned a verdict of 'accidental death' and Roberts and his companions walked free. Thanks to Hall, they and boxers ever since have been at liberty to inflict anything from cuts and abrasions to terminal knock-outs on each other, safe in the knowledge that the law stops short of the ropes.

Duke of Hamilton There are many factors which influence a man's choice of a wife. Some are captivated by a pretty ankle, others by a heaving bosom and a few have even allowed the lady's personality to have a bearing on the issue. But for this aristocratic old cricket buff nothing could beat the charms of a good square cut. So it must have been with a certain tingle of anticipation that he attended the cricket match for 'ladies of quality' organised by the Countess of Derby at the Oaks, Surrey in 1777.

Indeed it was fate. For when he saw Miss Elizabeth Ann Burrell get more notches in the first and second innings than any other lady in the game, it completely turned his head. He was so smitten with her performance at the crease that he proposed without delay and married her within the year.

A. Hamilton-Brown Losing the opening bout of the 1936 Olympic boxing tournament on a split decision was a bitter blow for this South African light-weight. He knew of only one way to console himself: he would go on a massive eating spree. After all the dieting and sweating to even make the weight for the games, it seemed like a good idea.

But while Hamilton-Brown was filling his face in a Berlin restaurant, a discrepancy had been found in the marking of his fight. One judge, it turned out, had inadvertently transposed his scores for the two boxers and so it was the South African, and not Lillo of Chile, that was the winner. Unfortunately by the time his manager caught up with him, Hamilton-Brown had gone the distance with several mountainous platefuls and was fit to burst. More to the point, for a man who had to fight the next day, he had put on nearly 5 pounds. He frantically tried to lose this excess baggage but it was no good. When it came to the weigh-in he was still over the limit and so was disqualified.

Mick Harfield According to his local paper in Hampshire, here was one of the greatest soccer enthusiasts of all time. For despite the fact that his young wife had died only hours before, he still turned out for his regular Saturday football side. Mr Harfield was not, however, a callous man and he had the decency to join his team-mates in observing two minutes' silence for his only-just-late spouse. So as not to intrude on the match itself this mark of respect was, of course, held at the half-time interval. As the *Romsey Advertiser* of 21 March 1975 remarked, 'The idea of Mick playing was to take his mind off the matter and he was a hero indeed to stay for the duration of the match.'

However, all was not as it appeared and in the next week's issue the following paragraph was published in the *Advertiser*, 'Mrs Rosina Harfield asks us to point out that references to her in the report of the Braishfield football match last week were completely untrue. She is fit and well and we would like to apologise to her for any upset the report could have caused.'

David Harris (b. 1754) The passage of time was not kind to this ancient Hampshire cricketer. In his hey-day he had been the greatest bowler in England but as the years advanced he became so plagued with gout that in the end even to stand was a trial. His long and glorious career seemed to be over. Harris, however, had other ideas and one of them was put into practice. So, whenever he felt like playing, a great armchair was wheeled onto the pitch and placed near the wicket for his convenience. After bowling each delivery, the old hero would take his seat and rest his suffering limbs upon its soothing upholstery, fielding, as it were, in the covers.

Revd J. T. Hartley (b. 1846) This tennis-playing clergyman surprised everyone, including himself, by reaching the last four of the singles at the Wimbledon Championships of 1879. However, as he came off court after his quarter-final victory on the Saturday, he realised that there was just one snag to his success. Because he had not anticipated getting so far he had made no provision for a substitute parson to take the following day's services at his parish of Durneston in the North Riding of Yorkshire. He was in a terrible fix. He did not want to scratch from Monday's semi-final but on the other hand his congregation 240 miles away were expecting to see him on Sunday morning all togged up at the altar.

There was only one thing for it. So, late on Saturday he took the train back to Yorkshire, wrote his sermon on the way and spent the following day leading his flock at their devotions. On the Monday he breakfasted at first light, drove a carriage ten miles to the station, reached London at two o'clock and arrived at Wimbledon just in time to dash onto court for his semi-final against C. F. Parr. But the huge round trip had taken its toll. Worn out by travelling and in dire need of a square meal, he played poorly and lost the first set 2-6. He looked to be on his way out of the championships.

It was then that the Great Umpire in the Sky, realising that one good turn deserves another, decided to intervene and down came the rain. The respite, and the refreshing cup of tea that he drank during it, was just the job. He emerged revitalised and won the next three sets in some comfort 6-0, 6-1, 6-1. In the final he was unstoppable, beating V. St Leger Gould in straight sets and the next year he defeated Herbert Lawford to retain the title. Although not a boastful man, the Revd Hartley could always claim, with some justice, to be the only Wimbledon champion never to miss a service.

Jim Hay An intrepid Scotsman, he twice risked life and climb for the sake of his golf. The first occasion was the Scottish Amateur Championship at Carnoustie in 1967. He came to his ball on the 14th to find that it had come to rest in the rough, just a couple of feet from a sinister-looking military object. The bomb presented him with a dilemma: to play the ball where it lay might prove fatal but the consequences of removing ball and self to a place of safety were even worse – he would collect a penalty shot. So, convincing himself that the thing was only a smoke bomb, he played the shot and the device remained mercifully un-detonated. This was just as well, because it later turned out to be a live mortar bomb.

Fifteen years on, Hay again featured at the same championships. The re-markable thing was that he was there at all. Three months earlier he had suffered a heart attack and his doctors had strongly advised him that he should play no more competitive golf. He ignored them and by sometimes playing two matches a day he actually managed to reach the quarter-finals.

Frank Hayes No matter how hopeless the cause this American jockey never spared any effort in his quest for victory. So, when he was lumbered with the 20-1 outsider Sweet Kiss in a race at the Belmont steeplechase meeting in July 1923, he rode as if it were his last race ever. It was. Hayes won but the strain of the finish proved too much and when the glad-handers and back-slappers pressed forward to congratulate him they found that he was slumped in the saddle, quite dead. His achievement of posthumously riding a winner is be-lieved to be unique.

Woody Hayes For 28 years this gridiron football coach had faithfully served Ohio State University. He had seen the good years and the bad, the ups and the downs and now here he was, watching them on one of their definite highs – the final of the 1979 Gator Bowl. Although they were two points down with only two minutes to go, Ohio were in possession and that, coach Hayes knew from his long experience, was what counted in this game. Yard by careful yard they advanced down the field when suddenly, an opponent intercepted a pass and Ohio's last chance was gone.

It was more than Hayes could stand. All his life he had just stood idly by whenever some thoughtless opponent wrecked his side's hopes, but this time he was going to darn well do something about it. He ran gibbering onto the pitch, seized Charlie Bauman the pass interceptor, punched him and then set about one of his own players who tried to intercede. Even by the standards of this muscle-bound sport, his behaviour was a little on the excessive side and after nearly three decades at Ohio he was sacked.

Jay Helgerson An American athletics addict who got hooked on running marathons. In 1979 he ran no fewer than 53 – more than one a week for the whole year. The extra race came when his regular fix was not enough and he ran two in one weekend.

Thomas Hicks This British-born professional entertainer won the 1904 Olympic marathon with the aid of some very strange substances indeed. The race, in the suburbs of St Louis, was held on an appallingly hot day and Hicks rather overdid the pace. By the 16 mile mark he was in a pitiful condition and near to collapse. Something of a reviver was called for. So his supporters administered generous quantities of cognac and, just for good measure, added some raw eggs laced with strychnine.

The awful cocktail worked. In medicinal doses sulphate of strychnine, as we should call it, is a quick-acting stimulant which induces a feeling of well-being. Within minutes Hicks was trotting off down the dusty road like a spring chicken. But the drug also sharpens the senses and after just six more miles his common sense told him that all was not well. In some distress he stopped and pleaded with his supporters to be allowed to retire. But having followed him round the course humping great quantities of eggs, brandy and strychnine, they were not prepared to see their afternoon's efforts go to waste. They gave Hicks a liberal dose of the special brew and sent him staggering on his way.

He had now taken on board more strychnine than his body knew what to do with and by the time he weaved his way into the stadium his central nervous system was in open revolt. It was all he could do to make the finishing line before passing out completely. He was six minutes ahead of his nearest rival and after a little contretemps with a hoax winner had been sorted out (see *Fred Lorz*), Hicks was declared the victor. But for all the comatose champion knew about it, he could have been declared Miss Pharmaceuticals of 1904. All attempts to revive him had failed and he was rushed to hospital, where the initial diagnosis was that he was now the late Olympic champion. Happily for him and the strychnine dispensers, he recovered. Just over a week later he was fit enough to receive a visit from Games officials who presented him with his gold medal in a moving little bedside ceremony.

Hinckley Athletic A Leicestershire soccer club who were so anxious to improve their form that on 20 April 1949 they fielded a team of hypnotised players.

The tactics were not a success and they lost their vital cup match against Bedworth Town 2-1.

Jemmy Hirst Early nineteenth century tycoon and sportsman. In his business dealings this Yorkshireman was a shrewd old cookie but when it came to anything else – including sport – he behaved like a fruitcake. This, and the large amounts of money he had to spend, made him a popular figure at racecourses which he always attended dressed in a shiny waistcoat made from drakes' feathers. When betting he would produce from its pockets a roll of banknotes of his own manufacture. These promised to pay the bearer on demand the sum of 5½d – an awkward amount but one which he was always willing to honour.

He also developed an unshakable belief that horses belonged in no other setting than the racecourse. So when he went shooting, his mount was a large bull and for pointers he employed a pack of pigs, all of whom answered to their own names. Given such a philosophy, it would have been quite wrong and disrespectful if he had undergone his final journey in a horse-drawn hearse. Lying in a coffin that he had purchased many years before, he was carried to his final resting place by eight widows who were paid half-a-crown each for their trouble. Following this courtege were a piper and fiddler playing a merry tune. It was a funeral rich in absurdities and the vast army of racing types, tipsters and sportsmen who showed up must have been pleased to see that Hirst, in the true traditions of the Turf, had saved his best until last.

Monty Holbein An adventurous old devil. At the age of 75 he swam the River Thames from Richmond to London Bridge, a distance of 16½ miles. It was the culmination of a remarkable sporting career which he had begun in the 1880s as a pioneer race walker and continued in spectacular fashion as a cyclist. In only ten years he broke no fewer than 32 national records, a quite absurd total, achieved, just for good measure, on four different types of bicycle. He was the first man to ride 20 miles in an hour on the road, the first to clock under six hours for 100 miles and, in numerous demolitions of the 24 hour record, he was the first rider to pass both the 300 and 400 mile marks.

A broken leg suffered in 1897 put paid to the pedalling and Holbein took to the water as a swimming enthusiast. Once he even attempted to cross the English Channel but having got to within 500 yards of Dover beach, the tide turned, he was swept out to sea and had to give up. Nevertheless he persisted with his swimming and eventually, after he had been drawing a pension for ten years, Holbein was able to go for his triumphant dip in the Thames.

Eleanor Holm The Olympic swimming champion who behaved so disgracefully on the way to the next Games that she was barred from defending her title. She was an American and had won the gold medal for the 100 metres backstroke at the 1932 celebration in Los Angeles. After the Games she kept herself in good enough trim to break the world record for the 100 and 200 metres in 1935 and 1936.

But her marriage in 1933 to singer and bandleader Art Jarrett had given her a fateful glimpse of the high life and when she saw how she and the rest of the American team would travel to the 1936 Games in Berlin she was not happy. Nine days in the third class bunks of the S. S. Manhattan was not Eleanor's idea of crossing the Atlantic. A first class cabin was more her style and without more ado she checked herself into one and plunged into the liner's social whirl.

For a swimmer about to undergo the supreme test she excelled herself: gambling, all-night drinking, being seen staggering along the deck in the company of a young man and even, at one point, yelling obscenities through a port-hole. It was a world class performance, a kind of medley relay of misbehaviour and the American team management, led by Avery Brundage, were appalled. They gave her repeated warnings but she ignored them. Finally, after she had enjoyed one particularly sensational night, they decided that Eleanor Holm should no longer feature in their Olympic plans. She was woken at 6 a.m. and told she was off the team. She went immediately to the stateroom of Brundage, no mean pleasure-monger himself on the quiet, and contested the decision through his locked door. But it was no use and the swimmer who had not been beaten for seven years spent the Olympics socialising.

She publicly challenged the winner of the 100 metres backstroke but it was never taken up and she returned to Hollywood. There, among other things, she appeared as Jane in a film called 'Tarzan's Revenge' where her leading man was someone who did get a medal in Berlin, decathlon champion Glenn Morris.

Dennis Horgan (1871–1922) A 17 stone Irish shot-putter whose natural brawn was enhanced before each competition by his habit of consuming a dozen eggs mixed into a mug of sherry. This repulsive aperitif helped him win no fewer than 13 Amateur Athletic Association championships, the last when he was 41. His greatest triumph, however, followed one of his rare failures. This was in 1900 when, having won the title for seven consecutive years, he was deprived of an eighth by US champion Richard Sheldon. Horgan was more than a little miffed and he decided to return the compliment and take his revenge in the American's own national championships.

They were then just over a month away and so he needed to move fast. He sent his entry without delay and began training harder than ever. No sacrifice was too great. He gave up his job and eked out his paltry funds by working his passage across the Atlantic on a cattleboat. Arriving in Boston the day before the contest, he travelled all through the night to New York and made it to the stadium in Manhattan Field just as the names of the shot-put competitors were being called. Sheldon and his compatriots were relaxing, confident that their burly Irish rival had not turned up. The judge continued announcing each entrant and in due course read out, 'Dennis Horgan, Ireland'. Instead of the expected silence a voice boomed out from the crowd, 'I am here.' With these words Horgan stepped into the arena, stole the show and won the championship with a throw of 46 feet 1¾ inches.

The rest of his career was hardly less dramatic. He won two more AAA titles in 1904 and 1905, returned to New York in 1907, worked as an auxiliary policeman, received terrible head injuries from a Bronx resident wielding a shovel, was patched up with a metal plate fitted in his skull, yet recovered to win four more AAA titles and an Olympic silver medal in 1908.

William Hoskins English merchant seaman and daredevil. On 20 December 1862 he had nothing better to do so he floated across the English Channel from Dover to Calais ensconced in a bundle of straw.

Henry Rupert Howell (1899–1984) Welshman, champion golfer and *bon viveur*, he was incited by some drinking cronies to play one of the most extraordinary rounds in golfing history.

It was June 1926 and Howell and his chums at the Glamorganshire Golf Club were whiling away the early evening in the bar when someone suddenly remarked that the day was of some significance. It was, he explained, the closing date for the Howell Cup, a trophy donated by the golfer's father for which members qualified by recording three good rounds. Howell, eight times Welsh champion and without doubt the premier player in the club, had already entered two impressive cards and was asked if he would be putting in a third. He ummed and aahed and said he might if a caddy could be found. While one was being located, Howell was asked to nominate a score and time for his round. 'A 72 in an hour and a half,' replied the great man, for he never liked life when it was too comfortable, and one of the assembly, knowing that Howell was also a gambling man, promptly offered him odds of 5-1 against the feat.

The prospect of easy money inflamed the company and very soon something of a public auction had developed. As each cry went up, the odds and the score grew ever more absurd – 6-1 on a 70 in 90 minutes, 10-1 on breaking 70 in 90 minutes and so on until one inventive soul even wagered him 40-1 on a 65 in 70 minutes. Howell took the lot.

Minutes later he drove from the first tee and marched smartly up the fairway, trailing a marker, timekeeper and a few energetic investors in his wake. Hole after hole followed in rapid succession and at each one he demonstrated his consummate skill and infinite local knowledge. The result was astounding – a 63 in 68 minutes. He was able to collect on every single bet.

R. L. 'Bonzo' Howland The greatest runner-up in athletics history. Starting in 1929, this Cambridge don began a heart-breaking sequence in the Amateur Athletic Association's shot-put championships which saw him finish second on no less than eight occasions and third twice.

I

Tony Incenzo A true football fan, he didn't just support one top club, but all 92 of them. By the age of 18 he had criss-crossed Britain several times and visited every ground in the Football League. Eighteen months later, in September 1982, he attended a game at Rangers' Ibrox Stadium to complete his collection of all 38 Scottish League clubs. By then his strange obsession, which also prompted him to watch the game at 150 non-League grounds and correspond with over 50 soccer pen-friends, had cost this student thousands of hard-earned pounds.

Indian Boys Athletic Association When this Calcutta League side came to their final Third Division match of the 1983 season they needed a really big win to avoid relegation. Even so, they did rather go over the top. A scoreline of 15-0 would have been perfectly adequate, 27-0 would have seen them home with a bit to spare and even 38-0 would not have aroused too much suspicion. But 114-0 was bound to attract attention. Sure enough, the League instigated an inquiry which probed, among other things, why this match against a side already relegated only lasted 70 minutes and produced a goal every 37 seconds.

Richard Ingerson An 11 handicap member of the Elfordleigh Golf Club in Devon who in 1983 achieved the unique trick of acing the same hole twice in one round. The explanation for this seemingly impossible feat is that his course consisted of nine holes played twice to make up the full round. He holed the 120 yard 2nd in one and then on his second circuit, playing the same green but from a tee set further back at 145 yards, holed out again.

Dimitris Iordanidis The astonishing old Greek is believed to be the world's oldest marathon runner. In 1976 at the age of 98 he ran from Marathon to Athens in 7 hours 33 minutes. He was apparently disappointed with his time, having completed the same course in 6 hours 42 minutes two years before.

Isadore Irandir A Brazilian goalkeeper whose attempt to gain a little divine intervention on his team's behalf came miserably unstuck. It was his habit to kneel in silent prayer in the goalmouth just before the kick-off. But when he played for Rio Preto against Corinthians at the Bahia Stadium he remained at his devotions a bit too long. Within three seconds of the start, Corinthians passed the ball to the dangerous Roberto Rivelino. Seeing that the goalkeeper was still deep in conversation with his Maker, Rivelino took aim and scored from the halfway line before Irandir could get to his feet. The keeper's brother obviously felt that the family honour had been besmirched, for he then ran onto the field with a revolver and fired six shots into the ball.

Vyachesla Ivanov The only Olympic champion ever to throw his gold medal away. It happened soon after the Russian rower had won the single sculls at the Melbourne Games of 1956. He was so delighted that after the presentation ceremony he danced a victory jig and threw his medal high into the air in jubilation. Up and up it went, down and down it came – right into the waters of Lake Wendouree. Ivanov was horrified. He dived in after it but despite searching for hour after hour he never found his precious medal. A team of professional divers were called in but after they failed the International Olympic Committee presented Ivanov with a duplicate. He went on to win more golds at Rome and Tokyo and made sure that he hung on tightly to those.

J

Marinko Janevski This retired Yugoslav policeman did not take kindly to interruptions when watching football on the television. One day his wife made the mistake of trying to turn off the set in mid-game. It was a fatal error, for Janevski strangled her and carried on viewing. At his subsequent trial for murder in 1982 he claimed that her actions were an extreme provocation and added, 'I always get excited when watching football.' The Belgrade court did not think that the circumstances were quite mitigating enough and found him guilty.

Giovanni Jans A kind of anti-sports nut. He was a barber from Hoeselt in Belgium who stood completely still for 10 hours 41 minutes one Friday night and Saturday morning in 1983. As a result of his 'efforts' he claimed a new world record for immobility.

Pope John XXII (c1321) Supreme Pontiff, Vicar of Rome, Holy father and closet football fan. He took the unusual step of granting papal dispensation to William de Spalding of England who was involved in a fatal football accident when an opponent fell against his knife during a game. Spalding could thus continue his soccer career free from any worries about excommunication.

Ernest 'Jonah' Jones (1869–1943) An Australian fast bowler who waged a peculiar campaign of psychological warfare against visiting England cricket teams. In his playing days he had taken 64 Test wickets at 29 runs apiece and after he retired his greatest pleasure was to ensure that the Poms were subjected to a torrent of abuse, even before they set foot on Australian soil. When the Englishman arrived by boat at Fremantle, he would row out in a dinghy and heckle them as they came into port. Once their ship was anchored, 'Jonah' would paddle round and round it, dropping his oars at regular intervals and yelling, 'Hundred to one, England for the Tests!'

Revd J.F. Jones Nineteenth century clergyman from Wolverhampton, he allowed his fundamentalist enthusiasm for football to somewhat colour his interpretation of the Bible. He once wrote, 'St Paul was such an admirer of physical games that were he alive now he would exercise his diligence to complete his week's work by mid-day on Saturday in order to witness a football match.'

K

Johnny Kelly An American runner who entered the 1928 Boston Marathon and enjoyed himself so much that in the next 55 years he only missed three of these races. He won the event in 1935 and 1945 and in 1982, at the age of 74, was still able to finish in a time of 4 hours 1 minute 18 seconds. A year later he completed his 52nd Boston Marathon.

Ralph Kennedy (1882–1962) The life of this American golfer was devoted to a restless search for the perfect golf course. For 52 years he maintained an average of playing a new course once every five days. By his death he had golfed over 3,615 different courses, and could prove it: for at each one he obtained an attested card witnessed by a club official.

Kennedy took up the game in September 1910 and soon began to appreciate the rich variety of terrain offered by golf. By 1932 he had played at his 1,000th club and thereafter there was no stopping him. Frantic bursts of exploration, like the month of October 1935 when he played at 31 different clubs in just 12 days, meant that by 1940 he had reached the 2,000 mark. The Second World War slowed him up a bit, but not a lot, and by 1951 the 69-year-old fanatic was able to step onto the first tee at St Andrews and claim the Old Course as his 3,000th. In the years that remained to him he visited another 615 clubs. By the end he could look back on playing golf in every state in the US, every province in Canada and in twelve other countries, including Bermuda, Cuba, Panama, Mexico, Colombia, Ecuador, Peru, Chile, Bolivia and Great Britain.

Les King A Norfolk golfer who caught a fish with a hook shot. It happened one day in 1983 when he drove from the 17th tee at Barnham Broom Golf Club. His shot was so wayward that it flew into a nearby river and brained a two foot long pike. Mr King said afterwards, 'I got the pike out of the water and there was a dent on the back of its head where the golf ball hit him. It is a unique golfing trophy and I am thinking of having it stuffed and mounted.'

Morris Kirksey An Olympic gold medallist, he was arrested and imprisoned before he had even had a chance to mount the victory rostrum. Up until then he had rather been enjoying the Antwerp Games of 1924 – helping the United States win the rugby tournament, winning a silver in the 100 metres and running in his country's triumphant relay squad. But just before the relay medals were due to be handed out by King Albert of the Belgians, Kirksey decided to nip back to the dressing room to collect his running kit.

When he got there the door was locked. Instead of being a sensible chap and waiting until the man with the keys came round, Kirksey made the mistake of trying to get through a window. Just at that moment a policeman passed by and seeing the lower half of the American poking out of the window, assumed the worst. The athlete was apprehended in what appeared to be mid-burgle, clapped in handcuffs and hauled off to jail.

Naturally he tried explaining. He also tried reasoning, pleading, protesting, demanding, grovelling and begging. It was no use, they could not understand English and he could not make head or tail of Flemish or French. When that had been established he tried sign language, waving his arms about and jumping up and down. It was still no good. Finally, after nearly 24 hours of this frustration, he was set free. He sped off to join his team-mates and their home-going liner and made it with only minutes to spare.

Joe Kirkwood An Australian showman, he played some of the most pre-posterous shots ever seen on a golf course. Simply hitting the ball a long way in a straight line never interested him. Instead he livened up the game by teeing up the ball on the face of a watch or a spectator's shoe and playing a full-blooded drive which left the impromptu tee unscathed. So well did he do it that he once holed in one from the face of a wrist watch.

He could also pound the ball into the ground so that only the top was visible and hit it 200 yards with a four wood, play left-handed with right-handed clubs and tee up six balls in a row and without looking, move down the line cleanly striking one after another, making them alternately slice and hook. Perhaps his greatest trick was to tee up two balls, hit them simultaneously with a seven iron

— 101 —

and make them cross in mid-air, one hooking the other slicing.

Kirkwood discovered this precious talent when, as the young Australian Open Champion, he was entertaining disabled World War One veterans in 1920. As he later recalled, 'I tried to show them what could be done even though they were amputees. I would hit a ball with one hand or standing on one leg.' So, although he later won four tournaments in the United States and twice finished fourth in the Open Championship, from then on he earned most of his money with Walter Hagen as the great man's sidekick and trick-shot specialist. Not, of course, that Hagen or Kirkwood needed to be on a golf course to get up to tricks. Once, when they were kicking their heels in a New York hotel, they decided to pass the time by playing the nearest thing they could find to a golf hole in Manhattan. Taking a club and ball each, they left the hotel, walked several blocks and stopped. The wager they then struck between them would go to whoever was first to play back to the hotel, through the lobby, up the lift, across the room and chip his ball into the toilet bowl. Hagen had won 11 major championships but with money on the shots and a lavatory pan to aim at, Kirkwood had no equal. He won with time and strokes to spare.

Ewa Klobukowska A Polish athlete who had the perfect answer to failing a sex test. A year or so after the chromosome counters at the 1967 European Cup Finals in Kiev had failed her and stripped her of her world record, she gave birth to a baby.

Violet Krahn A supple old lady, she was still competing in springboard diving events at the precarious age of 82. In her youth she had been a keen diver but had retired in 1928. However, the lure of the springboard proved too strong and after a break of only 50 years she made her comeback in 1978. Six years later this octogenarian's performance of the back dive with half twist was one of the highlights of the US Masters competition.

L

Ky Laffoon (b.1908) This American professional golfer was famous for the bizarre way he treated the tools of his trade. For instance, when he wanted to sharpen the leading edges of his irons, he would take the clubs into his car and, once he had reached sufficient speed, lean out of the window and grind the clubhead against the road.

That was when he was in a good mood. If he felt that any club had let him down he would not even let it travel inside the car. Once, after he had missed several crucial putts in a tournament, he tied the offending putter to his back bumper and trailed it clattering and scraping along the road all the way to the next event.

In his younger days Laffoon was something of a hustler. He teamed up with the notorious gambler 'Titanic' Thompson and worked an ingenious golfing sting on well-heeled but gullible opponents. The scam went like this: Thompson would arrange a match and appear on the first tee with Laffoon posing as his caddie. Little would the dupe suspect that the bag carrier was a player good enough to win eight US tour events and once finish fourth in the Masters.

Before the match was underway Thompson would start ragging his victim about his game and would always end his insulting routine with the words, 'Why, even my caddie could beat you.' The mug, stung to the core by being compared to the ramshackle figure at Thompson's side, would always accept the challenge, wager handsomely on the outcome and then watch in horror as the 'caddie' played like a pro. Exit Thompson and Laffoon all the way to the bank.

Charles Lamb An example of a sporting species long thought to be entirely mythical – the newspaper racing tipster who gets things right. On 28 July 1974 his column in the *Baltimore News American* gave a prediction for each of the ten races on the card at Delaware Park racecourse. Every single one of them was correct.

Arthur Lancefield The pseudonym of a lady tipster who frequented racecourses in the last century. She also went under the names of 'Mr Adelaide Merryweather' and, rather ominously, 'John Screwman'. When not in drag she posed as a 'disabled jockey's wife'. It was presumably in this guise that she tipped a winning double to a prosperous grain merchant who was so grateful that he married her.

W. Langstaff The inventor of the world's most disgusting golf ball. His brainchild was registered as British Patent No.16,488 in 1912 and the description of it contained the immortal words, 'The core of a golf, or other, ball consisting of a bull's penis, first prepared by skinning or drying.' One assumes that the secret was to wait until the animal had first died before attempting this rather delicate process. History, unfortunately, denies us any record of how this appalling projectile actually performed on the fairway.

George Larner (1875–1949) Champion walker whose training methods were, to say the least, unconventional. 'When circumstances permit,' this Brighton policeman said, 'all clothing should be removed for a run around a secluded garden, especially if it be raining at the time.'

This uncomfortable preparation was certainly effective. He won four Amateur Athletic Association titles in 1904 and 1905, retired, was tempted back for the 1908 Olympics where he won two golds, won a further AAA's title, retired again and made a final comeback to win the AAA championship at seven miles in 1911. This proved to be his last appearance. Perhaps by then he had moved to a house with a less secluded garden.

Gertrude Lawrence (1898–1952) A talented actress and lucky sportswoman. She had a hole in one with her first tee shot on her very first round of golf.

Monsieur Lenfant and Monsieur Mellant After big blow-out of a dinner there's nothing better than a nice quiet game of billiards. Or so these two Frenchmen thought. But no sooner had their match got underway one evening in 1834 than they began to bicker. At first it was little things, like the rules or

GERTRUDE LAWRENCE

Star of stage and green

what the score was, but then things really turned ugly. They began to argue about major issues, like how much money they had on the game and who had the chalk. Within minutes a blazing row was being conducted in high velocity French.

As the oaths and insults flew about M.Lenfant and M. Mellant could only agree on one thing: each had so besmirched the other's honour that there was only one way to obtain satisfaction – a duel. It was at this moment that they began to lose their sense of perspective. They were now so agitated that they could not wait for the usual pistols-at-dawn meeting with seconds in atten-dance. Instead they resolved to settle the matter there and then – with billiard balls at ten paces.

They solemnly drew lots to see who should fire first and M. Mellant won. Picking up the red ball from the table, he drew back his cuing arm, took careful aim and hurled the ivory missile straight between Lenfant's eyes, killing him instantly.

Battling Levinsky An American light-heavyweight who was so keen on boxing that he once had three fights in a single day. He started in Brooklyn with a ten round loosener against Bartley Madden, moved on to downtown New York and took on Soldier Kearns in another ten rounder before finishing off with a 12 round bout against Gunboat Smith in Waterburg. After that the rest of the day was his own. This hectic schedule certainly sharpened him up, for a year later, in 1916, Levinsky won the world title and held it for four years until he was knocked out by Georges Carpentier.

Mr A. J. Lewis Probably the worst golfer in the world. In a competition at Peacehaven, Sussex in 1890 he took 156 putts on one green – without holing out. Sadly his nerve broke before he could make his 157th wildly inaccurate jab with his putter and he was led shaking and mumbling from the course, never to return.

London Regiment, 18th Battallion The ultimate exponents of attacking football. They went over the top on 25 September 1915 at the First Battle of Loos and charged into no-man's-land kicking a ball between them.

Earl of Lonsdale (1857–1944) The peer of the realm who beat a world heavyweight boxing champion. This highly unlikely bout happened in the early 1880s when titleholder John L. Sullivan was touring the United States and offering to take on all-comers with the charmless boast, 'I'll fight anyone except pigs, dogs and niggers.' Lonsdale got to hear of this and having been tutored as a boy by the brawny hands of prizefighter Jem Mace, he thought he might just be the man to take Sullivan down a peg or two. He told a group of cronies that he fancied his chances and one of them, an actor with American connections called Hadyn Coffin, made contact with Sullivan. Before long, Lonsdale and his party were sailing for New York.

As a crowd-puller the bout would have matched any in history: Sullivan the vain, uncouth Irish-American champion against Lonsdale the English milord. But this was a private affair fought behind closed doors. The only spectators were each man's inner circle standing round the ropes at the secret venue, a riding school known as the Central Park Academy.

For the first round or two they stalked each other round the ring, testing and probing and trading a few investigatory punches. Then, in the third, Sullivan hit Lonsdale a fearful blow in the ribs. As Lonsdale later wrote, 'I thought I was done for . . . It took all the wind out of me and sent me staggering against the ropes.' But he hung on. By the fifth, even though his body was bruised and his left eye closed up, he got in 'several good stingers' and he noticed that Sullivan was breathing heavily.

At the opening of the sixth round Lonsdale decided that it was now or never and he heaved everything he could behind a right into the champion's stomach. Sullivan fell to the canvas and lay there immobilised until well after the count. The seemingly impossible had happened: the Earl of Lonsdale had beaten the Boston Strong Boy. But the victory was not without cost. When Lonsdale eventually shook hands with his opponent he felt a sudden piercing pain. He knew at once what it was. Despite the special gloves he wore – packed with human rather than horse hair – the force of that final telling blow had broken a bone in his right hand.

No man could have been more proud of an injury. But before he had finished with sport Lord Lonsdale had a lot more distinctions to take pride in. He won a 100 mile walking race, presented the Lonsdale Belts, was President of the National Sporting Club, raced the Kaiser in his yacht, competed at Cowes, fought many legal battles on behalf of boxing, was President of Arsenal Football Club, won coursing's Waterloo Cup, was the first President of the Automobile Association (who adopted his yellow livery as their own) and shot not only game but also tigers, buffalo and grizzly bears.

Then there were his equestrian achievements. He won the last six mile steeplechase to be run in England, was Chief Steward of the Jockey Club, owned the winner of the 1922 St Leger, was the founding spirit of the National Stud, was master of three hunts and started the Royal International Horse Show.

But merely devoting his life to competing, challenging and winning was not enough for Lonsdale, he always had to do everything in the grand manner. Other men hunted but only Lonsdale appointed his own Master of Horse. Others kept stables but only Lonsdale insisted that his coat of arms be laid out every morning in coloured chalks on the yard's fresh sand. Most aristocrats shot but only he gave his shooting dogs their own carriage on his private train. And when in middle age he entered the motor car era, he did so with consummate panache, racing round Brooklands in a Mercedes whose meticulous yellow paintwork required no fewer than 18 coats.

In fact, if it meant that he could lord it over his rivals then nothing was too much trouble or expense. When he took delivery of his first Mercedes he discovered to his horror that all the shiny bits were chrome and not silver as he thought. He sent the vehicle straight back to the factory with instructions that the chrome be replaced by the precious metal.

It was typical of Lonsdale. He had the income of an Earl but he lived and played like an Emperor. His cigar bill alone was £3,000 a year and apart from a Master of Horse he also maintained his own Chamberlain and Groom of the Bedchamber among his 100-strong staff. When he went on the move this vast liveried retinue went with him including, of course, his private 25 piece orchestra complete with their own Master of Music. If the entire household travelled at night by his train then it was the duty of his valet to remain awake and dispense largesse in the form of a £5 note to the station master of every station they passed through. No one could ever accuse Hugh Cecil Lowther, the 5th Earl of Lonsdale, of lacking style.

That style, and the wild extravagance that went with it, was the result of a headstrong nature that was apparent in him even as a boy. Apart from two years at Eton, which was about as much of him as the old school could handle, he was educated by a succession of private tutors. Few of them lasted long, most quickly surrendering to the futility of diverting their pupil from his sport. But one or two tried to inveigle their way into young Lonsdale's confidence by feigning an interest in his activities. In the case of a Monsieur Ciro this nearly proved fatal. Hugh took him on a river trip to demonstrate how to catch fish with a casting net, surreptitiously attached part of the line to the Frenchman's coat and so when the tutor flung the net, he also cast himself into the water. M.Ciro took to his heels for France the following day.

The answer to his wilfulness, his parents decided, was to send him to a finishing school in Switzerland. Hugh did not agree and within a month he had run away and joined a circus. He stayed with them for a year, until the news arrived that his father was prepared to make him an allowance of £1,200 a year.

He returned, took rooms in Jermyn Street and launched himself into the life of a young blood.

Being Lonsdale there were no half measures. If his fellows expected him to gamble then he would gamble and do so in considerable style. One night at the Duke of Devonshire's he excelled even himself, losing over £18,000 at the tables to unsavoury characters like 'Jubilee Juggins' Benzon and Sir Beaumont Dixie. He was bailed out by Lord Calthorpe, an old friend of the family, swore he would never gamble again and kept his word.

Sporting challenges, however, were another matter. His first one of any consequence was a walking match against Mr Weston, a famed American pedestrian. The course was from Knightsbridge barracks right up the Great North Road to the Ram Jam Inn beyond Stamford, a distance of 100 miles. They started on the evening of 17 June 1878 and the powerful Lonsdale soon strode ahead. He stopped briefly three times an hour to catch his breath, changed his socks and shoes every five miles but still managed to win the race in an admirable 17 hours 21 minutes. He then nonchalantly strolled on up to Ashfordby for dinner with his mother.

His other great challenge was a driving match against the Earl of Shrewsbury. The race was to be in four stages (buggy, trap, four-in-hand, and open phaeton) over the 20 miles from Dorking to Reigate. The stake was £100 but the ever-competitive Lonsdale spent over £6,000 on horses, carriages and special harnesses in his bid to win it. In the event Shrewsbury did not arrive at the start but Lonsdale drove over the course in 54 minutes and claimed victory. He was then summoned by the local magistrates for 'furious driving on the highway.' The case was dismissed but the bad blood between him and Shrewsbury, stoked by the threat of libel writs, rumbled on for years.

His ability to sustain a dispute was indeed legendary. He once rowed with the Earl of Derby for five solid years about whether there should be an extra lavatory in the Ladies at Newmarket. For the most part these quarrels were the result of his obstinacy but a contributory cause was his somewhat simplistic view of human nature. He once said, 'I can tell everything I want to know of a man by the way he sits on a horse.' Sophisticated he was not and when he came to raise a private regiment during the Great War he issued a recruiting poster in his racing colours which posed the question, 'Are you a man who will forever be handed down to posterity as a gallant patriot or as a rotter and a coward?'

There was never any danger of Lonsdale being branded by history as a coward. After all, hadn't he, besides everything else, also conquered the North Pole, discovered the Klondike, wrestled with grizzly bears, saved the Cheyenne stagecoach from outlaws and visited Rasputin in a Siberian prison? Well no, actually he hadn't. But that did not stop him adding these yarns to his life story when he sold it to the *People* newspaper for £16,000 in 1937.

He just could not help himself, even his lies had to be on a lavish scale. And that was what was really so stylish about him. He had no need to lie, so he did; he was not nearly so rich as he pretended, so he spent wildly; there was no reason for him to box, race and compete, but he could not resist doing so. All that the Earl of Lonsdale ever required to know was that there was a bit of sport in something. If there was, then that was always good enough for him.

Valentin Loren This featherweight boxer was desperate to make a name for himself at the 1964 Tokyo Olympics and he didn't much care how he did it. Fouling with his head and holding his first round opponent, Formosan Cheng Hsu – there was almost no limit to Loren's underhand tactics. But after not much more than a minute the Hungarian referee, Gyorgy Sermer, had seen enough dirty work and he disqualified the Spaniard.

Loren was outraged and it was then that something in him snapped. If he could not beat his opponent, he decided, he would at least have the satisfaction of beating the referee. So he turned on Sermer and crashed a left hook into his face. Then, when a Netherlands judge tried to intervene, the angry little fighter hit him as well. It was the last punch he ever landed, for the boxing authorities subsequently banned him from the sport for life.

Fred Lorz The perpetrator of the most notorious hoax in the history of the Olympics. At the 1904 Games in St Louis he managed to fool thousands of people, the President's daughter, countless officials and even, for a few moments, himself into believing that he had won the marathon. It was, however, all a joke that had got rather badly out of hand.

Lorz had started the race with the best of intentions and actually led for a while. But around the nine mile mark he developed cramp so badly that he was forced to drop out and hitch a lift from a passing truck. Then, as he rode back towards the stadium, the cramp gradually wore off. So when the vehicle broke down with five miles to go he decided that he may as well run the rest of the way and off he trotted.

Now, he knew he had taken a lift but the crowd lining the route didn't. When Lorz hove into view, fresh as a daisy, they thought he was winning and began cheering, waving flags and shouting encouragement. He would have stopped and explained but, if the truth be told (which it wasn't until much later), he was rather enjoying himself. So much so that when he reached the arena the sight and sound that greeted him quite turned his head.

He smiled as the crowd roared at his entry into the stadium, waved in acknowledgement of their sustained cheering and raised his hands aloft as he broke the tape in triumph. He was having such a good time that he saw no reason why he should not bask in this passing glory for just a few moments more. So he stood there, modestly accepting the congratulations and backslapping that showered upon him. But when he saw President Roosevelt's daughter Alice advancing towards him, public-appearance grin in place and laurel wreath and medal in hand, he must have begun to think that perhaps the time had arrived for a full and frank confession.

It was not to be, for at that instant other runners began to finish. Without even stopping to catch their breath they converged on the 'victor' and confronted him with the truth. He gave a wan smile and admitted all. It was, he told the officials, just his little joke. But they didn't laugh, instead they awarded the race to Thomas Hicks and banned Lorz for life. He was, however, nothing if not resourceful and the following year he entered the Boston Marathon and was allowed to run. He won and this time he ran all the way – honest.

P.B. 'Laddie' Lucas An adventurous sportsman who, for reasons best known to himself, once played a round of golf while blindfold. The course was Sandy Lodge in Hertfordshire and his sense of direction was so acute that he scored an 87. This, however, was no ordinary golfer. Five years previously, in 1949, Lucas had captained Britain's Walker Cup side and had also, in his time, won the President's Putter.

Randolph Lycett This Australian tennis player was so anxious to make an impression at Wimbledon in 1920 that he had a liveried waiter serve him champagne between games. The result was inevitable – he lost and had to be carried off the court. In his subsequent visits to the tournament he let his tennis do the impressing and he won the men's doubles three years in a row.

Jack Lynch Irish Prime Minister, Gaelic gamesman of the highest class and the only known sports record holder to become a head of government. He played hurling and Gaelic football for his native Cork and was the first man to win six successive All-Ireland senior championship medals and was also the first to play in seven consecutive finals. He also represented Munster at both sports in inter-provincial finals on the same afternoon.

George Lyons (1858–1938) The only man ever to refuse an Olympic gold medal. He had travelled to Britain in 1908 to defend the golf title he had won at the St Louis Games four years before. But when he arrived he found that his rivals – all British – had withdrawn owing to some tedious internal dispute. He was offered the gold yet sportingly refused it. Since golf has featured in no further Games he is still, therefore, the reigning Olympic golf champion.

Lyons, a Canadian, is indeed a worthy champion – not least because he caused something of a stir at the 1904 presentation dinner by walking the length of the dining room on his hands. The real wonder is that he became so good at golf, for he did not take up the game until a comparatively advanced age. In his youth he had been too occupied with cricket (his innings of 238 is a Canadian record), baseball, tennis, football, curling and rowing. So he was 38 before he first held a golf club and yet within two years he had won the first of eight Canadian Amateur Championships.

M

Mad Mac A curious caddy. Whatever the weather his attire on the golf course always consisted of a raincoat, but never a shirt. It was also his practice to study the contours of the greens through binoculars from which the lenses had been removed. For many years he carried the clubs of Max Faulkner and once, when the 1951 Open Champion was faced with an awkward putt, he delivered the immortal line, 'Hit it slightly straight, sir.'

Kid McCoy (1872–1940) This American boxer played a confidence trick on an opponent and so gave the English language a new expression, for this plausible rogue was the original 'real McCoy'.

It all started in 1896 when he was booked to fight Tommy Ryan for the world welterweight crown. Fearing that he might not win without a little assistance, McCoy hit on a brilliant but underhand scheme: he would make Ryan feel sorry for him. So he fed the boxing grapevine with the pathetic story that he had consumption and was only fighting in this debilitated condition because he needed a big purse to pay the doctor's bills. He even powdered his face so that it had an authentically consumptive pallour.

Ryan fell for the yarn completely. He didn't bother to train and, by the time he entered the ring, felt more like organising a whip-round for the 'invalid' than fighting him. Imagine his surprise, therefore, when in the first round McCoy leapt from his corner and began jigging and jabbing like a man possessed. Ryan realised he had been conned but it was too late and he was knocked out in the 15th round. Thus the title went to McCoy – not the pasty-faced, consumptive version but the 'real McCoy' as people began calling him. For a con-artist like the Kid the expression was the supreme tribute, especially as his name was not McCoy at all. The real McCoy was really Normal Selby.

Perhaps his cheekiest trick was played on Frenchman Jean Charlemont. They were fighting in Paris and McCoy was in trouble. Until, that is, the sight of a pretty girl in the crowd gave him an idea. The next time he got close to Charlemont he told him there was a real cracker sitting down there among the boxing fans. Then, as the Frenchman turned to look at this beauty, McCoy knocked him out. Later, when Charlemont protested in the dressing room, McCoy told him, 'Never let a woman turn your head.'

It was advice that McCoy was well-placed to give, for he was married no less than eight times. In between wives he boxed all over the United States and Europe and even, at the Wonderland arena, London in 1909, took on three men in one night. It was a typical McCoy performance. He knocked two of them out, had a third disqualified and did all this while fighting in his street clothes. Finally, at the age of 43, after holding one world title, challenging for another and dubiously claiming a third, he retired. McCoy then turned to Hollywood and used in films the acting talent that had served him so well in the ring. He committed suicide in 1940.

Father John Archie MacMillan Scottish priest and daredevil, he became convinced that it was possible to water ski and play the bagpipes at the same time. So in June 1982 on the Sound of Eriskay in the West Highlands, he put his theory to the test. Wearing a special harness that kept his hands free for the pipes, he water skiied for three miles up and down the Sound while playing selections from 'The Steamboat', 'Oh Susannah' and 'The Argyll's Crossing the River Po'. His recital was a great popular success – proof indeed that this instrument is best enjoyed when the audience is on dry land and the piper is heading out to sea.

Rajah of Manipur Sporting Indian potentate who went to war with the neighbouring province of Cachar – to recover a stolen polo pony. He was not a naturally aggressive man and had put up with all the sackings, rapings, pillagings and other liberties that Cachar had taken down the years. But pinching his favourite polo mount was going too far and he launched a full-scale military assault to get it back. Despite the ensuing carnage his subjects were right behind him. After all, their enthusiasm for the game was such that some players were known to have pawned their wives to buy a pony.

Gerhard Marinell A very fortunate Austrian sky-diver, he survived a 3,300 feet descent without a parachute. He had not intended to come down the hard way but when he leapt from an aeroplane one afternoon in 1983, his chute simply failed to open. The 42-year-old plunged through nearly a mile of thin air and crashed onto a roof in Soelden near Innsbruck before falling into the garden below. The cost of this hasty return to earth was just three broken ribs.

Dao Marino The only grandfather ever to win a world boxing championship. An Hawaiian, he took the flyweight title from Terry Allen in 1950. He was then aged 34 with his household already into their third generation.

'Mr Martin' A gentleman gambler who was so keen to win on the horses that he invented a racecourse, held a 'meeting' there, got his pals to bet on its fictitious results and nearly, very nearly, got away with it all.

The case of the course that never was began in late July 1898 when a man in a black topper entered the London offices of the *Sportsman*, a leading sporting daily of the time. He asked the editor to publish the card for the Trodmore hunt Steeplechases, due to be run on August Bank Holiday Monday. The man was well spoken, gave his name as Martin and helpfully offered to provide full details of the meeting and even to telegraph the results. The editor, a trusting soul, agreed to the request and on the morning of the meeting the card duly appeared in the paper's columns.

'Mr Martin's' confederates then went into action. Clutching copies of the *Sportsman*, they toured London betting clubs and pubs and wagered heavily on a horse called Reaper which was down to run in Trodmore's fourth race. Lo and behold, when the results were published on the morrow there among the Trodmore winners was Reaper at the handsome price of 5-1. The happy band of swindlers set off to collect their winnings. It was then that they hit a snag. The bookmakers, never content at the best of times to pay out, refused to do so now until the results had also been published in the *Sporting Life*. 'Mr Martin' was not to be denied. He contacted the *Life* and they printed the results exactly as 'Mr Martin' dictated them.

Well, almost exactly. For a printer's error now gave Reaper at the less advantageous price of 5-2. The bookies, ever hopeful that this was the correct version, sought confirmation that this was so and began to make inquiries. At first they asked innocent little questions like, what were Reaper's odds and what was the time of the race? Then, however, more pertinent queries came to be made, including the baffling one, 'Where the hell is Trodmore?' Soon it was apparent to bookies and newspapers alike that there was no Reaper, no meeting and, more to the point, no Trodmore. When the police began their investigation there was no 'Mr Martin' either. He and his associates had left no more trace than their mythical racecourse.

Mrs Paddy Martin This lady golfer had an extraordinary Easter in 1960. Playing at Rickmansworth Municipal Golf Club, Hertfordshire, she holed in one at the 125 yard third on Good Friday, repeated the performance on the Saturday and on Easter Monday did it yet again. Each ace was achieved with the same club and the same ball at the same hole.

Mary Queen of Scots (1542-1587) Catholic champion, sometime pretender to the English throne and history's first recorded golf enthusiast. Such was her devotion to the game that she was seen playing it in the grounds of Seton House just two days after her husband Darnley's murder in 1567. Her action was widely criticised at the time, few people then understanding the benefits of golf at times of stress. Mary knew better. She had learnt a version of the sport while at school in France so that when she returned to govern Scotland in 1561 she already had the rudiments of a swing. A famous picture shows her poised over a particularly awkward bunker shot at St Andrews in 1563. As a few attendants cower at a prudent distance, their young monarch addresses the ball with what looks suspiciously like a slicer's grip.

Sport was indeed a constant source of comfort to this unhappy lady who, it seemed, could hardly poke her nose outside the front door without either losing a husband or being imprisoned. Life, however, is seldom fair and in time she was to be robbed even of the solace of her games. In 1576, while being held under arrest by Elizabeth, her captors took Mary's beloved billiard table away and despite her complaints about this 'cruelltie', they kept it from her. Subjected to this and other forms of subtle torture, she died 11 years later.

Norman Mate An 84-year-old pensioner, he took part in a 12½ mile road running race – entirely by accident. There was old Norman, out for his morning stroll and minding his own business, when he came across a charity run being staged near his home in Trentham, Stoke. He agreed to pay a £1 entry fee and trot along in the mile race but he had forgotten his hearing aid and misheard the starting instructions. So instead of joining the mile entrants, he lined up alongside a field of club athletes competing in a half marathon. Off they went and before Norman had got into his stride his fellow competitors had disappeared over the horizon. Undaunted, he plodded on and on and on, uphill and down dale, past feeding stations and checkpoints. All the while he was still

MARY, QUEEN OF SCOTS

Billiard player and Pretender to the throne

neatly turned out in his lounge suit and walking shoes. Finally, hours later on that day in 1983, he crossed the finishing line, having travelled no fewer than 11½ miles further than he intended.

Ted Matson This American was so hard up for opponents at table tennis that he taught his cat Dagwood to play the game. Instead of a bat the animal used his paw and was, of course, allowed to stand on the table. Henceforward no morning at the Portland, Oregon home of these two ping-pong fans was complete without a match between man and beast.

Mr Matthews An imaginative promoter of women's cricket. In 1890 this showman hit upon the novelty of organising a touring team of female players. He placed a newspaper advertisement for suitably accomplished ladies and was delighted to receive such an enthusiastic response that he was able to raise not one but two teams. He rapidly set about making the arrangements, which naturally included engaging the services of a chaperone, and within a short while Mr Matthews was able to get his bizarre show on the road.

Billed as 'The Original English Lady Cricketers', they toured the country that summer, subsisting on 6d a day pocket-money each and playing exhibition matches at several of the larger grounds. Wherever they went they attracted vast crowds, most of whom were drawn as much by the prospects of seeing a flash of calf as they were by any skill that might be on display. Indeed, turned out in their rather fetching red or blue uniforms, the cricketers in skirts presented an easy target for all manner of ribald remarks and lurid suggestions.

Perhaps it was to prevent these and other unwanted attentions continuing after the close of play that led Matthews to insist from the start that none of his ladies were to play under their own names. A wise precaution maybe, but one which rendered the scorecard a fiction from beginning to end. The captain of the first eleven, for instance, was always referred to as 'Miss Flora Lynn' but she was in fact a Mrs Westbrook. Yet despite the good crowds and the pleasure – innocent or otherwise – that they provided, the Original English Lady Cricketers were disbanded at the end of that season. They never re-grouped. Mr Matthews' bold experiment was at an end and his ladies remain to this day the only recorded female cricket professionals.

Edward J. May (1910–1954) The bravest, or possibly the most foolhardy, long distance swimmer in history. In 1954 this Scunthorpe boilermaker became the first man to try and swim the English Channel alone, without any accompanying boats or support. His experiences ensured that he was also the last to ever make such an attempt.

Up until that summer May was just one of the many characters on the fringes of the Channel swimming world. At 17 stone and six foot tall he had the build to last the distance but he was slow and because of this had twice been refused entry into the Cross-Channel race. These rebuffs were the motivation behind his solo attempt. 'I wanted to show them I could do it without their assistance,' he said.

The decision to go it alone was one no swimmer had ever dared consider before. The Channel is a very treacherous stretch of water indeed. It is the busiest shipping lane in the world and jellyfish, oilslicks and seaweed are just some of the hazards of crossing it. But besides these, the seasickness and fatigue, what really intimidates the swimmer are the tides. They can turn a nominal crow's-flight distance of 22½ miles into a zig-zagging haul of anything up to 45 miles that can take as long as 25 hours to complete. Even with medical men, feeders, trainers and, above all, experienced pilots in attendance, 225 of the 260 attempts before 1950 had failed.

Despite these appalling odds and the pleadings of the French authorities, May was determined and during August he prepared as best he could. Realising that he would have to feed himself, he made a pannier from a large coffee tin and fitted this inside an inflated car inner-tube. Into the pannier he put a compass, two bottles of rum, sliced chicken, sugar and biscuits. On the morning of 23 August the 44-year-old padded down the beach at Cap Gris Nez and entered the water with his pannier strung out behind him.

For quite a time all went well. Even after five hours, when he felt hungry and pulled in his supplies only to find that the chicken and biscuits had been washed away, it seemed no more than a minor irritant. He simply uncorked the rum and took a long swig. May swam on for another hour and when the white cliffs of Dover came into view in the far distance he felt a surge of excitement. 'My confidence was greater than ever,' he said later, 'the sun was shining and the sky was clear.'

Suddenly the weather changed. Black clouds rolled over, a strong wind sprang up and down came the rain. The tide had switched and he knew then that he would not make it to England. So, turning his back on those famous cliffs, he headed back towards France.

By this time the authorities had been alerted by his failure to appear anywhere near the shore and had launched a search. Two British destroyers, helicopters, planes, Channel traffic and the coastguards were all scanning the ocean for him. It was a seemingly hopeless task. They were trying to find a target no bigger than a man's head and upper arms in the shifting grey mass of the sea. It did not help that May was now headed in the opposite direction to that expected. There was only one real chance – that he would find them – and by some miracle he did. Two hours after reversing course and with tiredness creeping over his body and despair sneaking into his mind, he saw the masts of a ship on the horizon. He stepped up his strokes, shouted and waved and by great good fortune the crew of the Finnish steamer spotted him. Within minutes he was being pulled on board.

He was bitterly disappointed at his failure and in spite of coming so near to death he began planning his next attempt as soon as he reached dry land. He did not even let a road accident the very next day, which put him in hospital, hold him up for very long. Soon he was back in France and raring to go, but the French had other ideas. They seized his passport at Calais and phoned Paris for instructions. Much to their regret, the Ministry of the Interior replied that there was no law to prevent May's second bid, all that could be done was to warn him that he might well be going to his death. May refused to listen. The only concession he would make to safety was to fit his inner-tube with a metal mast on which were fixed two lights.

In the early hours of 8 September he stood on the beach at Cap Gris Nez, prepared once more to go it alone. He seemed to spend some minutes hesitating on the shore but at 4.30 a.m. he stripped to his trunks, put on goggles, a bathing cap and three layers of grease, fitted a compass to his wrist and plunged into the sea. He swam off strongly but as the day wore on no sign was seen of him. Concern mounted and by early evening, with waves six feet high and the wind gusting at 30 mph, a full-scale search was underway. It involved the Dover and Walmer lifeboats, RAF and United States Air Force planes, coastguards, high speed rescue boats and nearly a dozen other craft. All Channel shipping was radioed to be on the alert and even US warships and their helicopters were put on standby.

At last a sighting was made. The crew on board the British tanker San Vito saw a man in the sea four miles southeast of the South Goodwin lightship. As they closed in they could see him desperately waving his arms and calling for help. The chief officer threw a lifebelt but it fell 20 yards short of the flailing figure. The ship turned to come in again but by the time they returned the belt was floating empty on the waves and the man was nowhere to be seen. On and on through the night the San Vito and the rest of the rescue fleet looked for sight or sound of May, but none came. Nor was there a trace of him the following morning and gradually they realised that it was pointless continuing.

Several weeks later the body of May was washed ashore on the sands near

Burgen in Holland. His compass was still strapped to his wrist. The boilermaker from Scunthorpe who tried to beat the sea all on his own had at last been found. He left a widow and nine children.

Vince Mazzey As the 1983 season drew to its climax this American football fan was desperate to see his favourite team, the Miami Dolphins, play in Los Angeles. So desperate, in fact, that when he found out that all direct flights between the two cities were fully booked, he did not mind making a slight detour – to another continent. He made it to the game, having flown from Florida to Los Angeles via London, a round trip of some 12,000 miles.

'Melpomene' Energetic Greek girl who assumed a false name, dressed up as a man and ran in the first Olympic marathon in 1896. There was, however, no disguising her ladylike pace in the all-male event and she took four and a half hours to finish. It was 88 years before women were officially allowed to compete in a marathon at the Games and the winning time then was two hours faster than 'Melpomene's'.

Mental's Only Hope An extremely enthusiastic greyhound. He was enjoying himself so much in the 8.15 at Wimbledon Stadium in March 1961 that when the race stopped, he didn't. Instead he just kept going, round and round and round. Officials waved at him, kennel lads and lasses tried to intercept him but it was all to no avail. No one could tempt the runaway in for a pit-stop. Finally, after 30 minutes and 29 seconds of circling the track he came to a halt, dog-tired.

Joseph Merlin Belgian musical instrument maker and roller-skate pioneer. He unveiled the first pair in the world in a dramatic demonstration at a grand social masquerade at Carlisle House, Soho Square in 1760. For some reason he was convinced that his entrance would have additional impact if he was playing the violin at the same time. So while the guests milled around at the function Merlin repaired to an ante-room, fitted the skates, picked up his fiddle and took an almighty run-up.

At the vital moment the ballroom doors were flung open and the wheeled Merlin shot in to the accompaniment of his own vigorous tune. He flew across the floor picking up speed on its polished surface and it was only then, when he reached maximum velocity, that it occurred to the test pilot that he had no idea how to turn or slow down, let alone stop. His panic was not eased when he looked up and saw an identically dressed violinist hurtling towards him from the opposite direction. Too late did he realise that it was his own reflection in the full-length ballroom mirror. Crash went the looking-glass, smash went the violin and Merlin himself was all but killed.

His misadventure set back the cause of roller-skating 83 years for it was not until 1823 that the first remotely safe pair of skates were introduced. Their inventor, a Piccadilly fruiterer named Robert Tyres, also had the good sense to test them on a tennis court, well away from any mirrors.

Milo of Croton The greatest – and hungriest – of all the original Olympic champions. At five consecutive Olympiads from 536 BC to 520 BC he won the wrestling and would, if there had been such a thing, have won the greedy guts competition as well. Each day he was said to eat 20 pounds of meat, 20 pounds of bread and drink 18 pints of wine. The climax to his career as a champion strongman and nosebagger came with one startling exhibition at Olympia. He was reported to have run round the stadium carrying a four-year-old bull on his shoulder, then killed it with a single blow and eaten all the edible parts within a day.

Captain Mingaud In the late eighteenth century this French army officer became convinced that the equipment for the game of billiards was sorely in need of improvement. He was sure he could come up with some refinements, if only he had plenty of spare time and a laboratory where he could work undisturbed. All at once these conditions were provided. The French authorities threw him into the Bastille. It was perfect and after somehow managing to have a billiard table installed in his cell, he spent his incarceration in a ceaseless search for a better cue. He was so absorbed in his work and so well treated that when the time came for his release the billiards boffin asked for permission to stay on in prison and continue his experiments there.

Eventually, about 1790, the breakthrough came. In a flash of inventive genius he rounded off the square end of the cue and was thus able to play shots the like of which had never been seen before. Only then did he consent to his liberation. Once at large the captain spent most of his free time playing and in 1807 he completed his life's work when he further improved the cue by adding a leather tip to the rounded end.

Gloria Minoprio This trained conjuror featured in one of the most mystifying performances ever given on the sporting stage. It happened at the 1933 English Women's golf Championship when she not only appeared with her face made up in a haunting white mask but also used just one club for every shot, including the putts. As if that was not enough to attract attention, she increased the effect by playing in trousers – an act then considered only marginally less scandalous than playing without any clothes at all – and seemed to be in some kind of trance, speaking not a word to anyone throughout the entire round.

What was especially baffling was that she never offered one word of explanation for her peculiar behaviour. At the end of her match, which she lost 5 and 4, she got into her car and sped away. In the absence of any enlightenment from the lady herself, speculation began. Some thought it was all a publicity stunt, but this theory was somewhat devalued by her failure to make any attempt to cash in on the hoo-ha that followed her appearance. Others, latching onto her zombie-like state and the rumour that she had once studied yoga in India, argued that she played while under hypnosis.

Meanwhile, the Ladies Golf Union were less interested in why she did what she did than the fact that she did it in trousers. And not only trousers, for her rig-out also consisted of a turtle-neck sweater and woollen cap, all in a fetching shade of navy blue. Appalled at such fancy dress, the LGU issued a statement saying that they 'deplored any departure from the traditional costume of the game.' At the time this was taken to be the following: a rather mannish white shirt, collar and tie, a shapeless cardigan shrewdly designed to give the impression that the bust occurred somewhere around the midriff, a dowdy skirt, thick socks or heavy-duty guage stockings and two-tone golf shoes. The outfit was topped off with the kind of beret made popular by onion sellers. Small wonder, then, that the LGU found Miss Minoprio's ensemble such a shock.

Much to their relief nothing more was heard of this strange lady. Until next year's championship that is, when she appeared in exactly the same manner as before. Again she lost in the first round. So it went on for another three years: out of the car she would step in her golfing trousers and bleached complexion and then, armed always with one club, she would proceed to play her way silently round the course and lose. It was a miracle that she kept her matches alive as long as she did, for the solitary club she used was a two-iron, an implement designed to hit the ball low over long distances but utterly useless for chipping over bunkers, or indeed out of them.

On her sixth appearance in the championship she actually won a match but even then it was the same story – off in her car without ever a syllable of explanation. When she finally departed that year, after the second round, it was for the last time. This extraordinary apparition never showed her pasty face in public again.

Minoru A Derby winner and the only racehorse ever to be tried and convicted as a political criminal. In his youth this magnificent animal was owned by King

MINORU

Derby winner and political martyr

Edward VII and wearing the royal colours he won the Derby and Two Thousand Guineas in 1909. After his racing career ended he was exported to Russia where he enjoyed a few merry years running around a stud farm paddock and 'covering' any mare he could lay his fetlocks on.

Then in 1917 came the Russian Revolution. The Bolsheviks, frantically trying to make up for centuries of being down-trodden, left no quarter of privilege unturned and it did not take them long to get round to the nobility's farms and studs. These they seized and every mare and foal they could find was rounded up and burned with petrol. But a horse like Minoru, with particularly elitist connections, was dealt with more formally. The fanatics found the old Epsom winner in his stable, took his reins and led him into town where he was tried by a 'court martial' for crimes against the proletariate. The outcome of this legal farce was a foregone conclusion. Unable, of course, to defend himself, let alone enter a plea of mitigation, he was found guilty, condemned to death, taken to the market square and summarily beheaded.

Bob Montgomery Football fan who tried to get his club taken to court for their lack-lustre performance in an FA Cup replay. He felt that Sheffield Wednesday's game against Southend in 1983 bore so little relation to football that it was an offence under the Trades Description Act. He even asked the local consumer watchdogs to intervene. 'What I saw was not football,' he fumed, 'it was a shambles. It was obtaining money by false pretences.' The disgruntled fan also demanded a refund of his entrance money but this, and the request for a prosecution, was rejected.

Shirley Morgan The wife of a club cricketer, she put 21 men to shame one crazy afternoon in 1983. She had arrived at the Mountain Ash ground in Mid-Glamorgan to watch her husband play, but before Mrs Morgan had time to settle into her deckchair she was told that his side were one short and was offered a game. It was her big chance and she took it, opening the innings with a top score of 51, taking two wickets for 21 runs in six overs and holding a catch.

It was obvious from her match-winning display that Shirley was no beginner but that did not stop the men's blushes. Her husband Gary, who could manage only 15 runs, said afterwards, 'She is a much better cricketer than me. I took a lot of ribbing from the boys – but not as much as the opposition bowlers did when she hit 51 off them.'

David Morgan One evening in the summer of 1983 this golf club greenkeeper padded down to the shore of Loch Ness, stripped to his swimming trunks, put on his cap and goggles and slipped into the water. It was bitterly cold and as he swam on and on that night the Loch's temperature was never more than a dozen degrees above freezing. Not that Morgan was deterred by that, or by the distance of 24 miles he had to cover before he got to the other end of the loch. He ploughed on and after just 9 hours 57 minutes of moonlit swimming, he made it.

But the task that the 19-year-old Yorkshireman had set himself was far from over. He allowed himself a ten minute break, during which he re-fuelled with two rounds of salami sandwiches, two apple pies, chocolate and a pint of coffee, then returned to the water and began the long swim back to where he had started. He was not swimming so fast now. The cold and lack of sleep were sapping his strength, making the rough and ready comforts of the accompanying boat seem more inviting than he had ever known. But he resisted, kept on swimming and finally reached his goal. The entire 48 mile swim had taken him 23 hours 5 minutes but his time was largely irrelevant, for no other human being had ever before swum Loch Ness two ways.

Achieving extraordinary feats in water had been a regular feature of Morgan's life since he was ten years old. At that age, while most of his contemporaries were struggling to cope with a width of the local swimming baths, he swam the eight miles from Filey to his native Scarborough. Within two years he had conquered three of the toughest English Lakes – Windermere, Coniston and Ullswater – and by 13 he had become the youngest-ever person to swim the English Channel. In the years that followed he collected the records for rivers, lakes and oceans like most young men collect stamps.

His most outrageous performance came in 1984 whe he was 20. He had gone to the west Coast of America to swim the Catalina Strait, the treacherous 23 mile stretch of the Pacific between the island of that name and the California mainland. It was an intimidating prospect. But although he knew about the tides, the heat and the sharks, they did not bother him. What did disturb him, and in a fairly major way, was the left arm he had damaged earlier that year attempting a three-way crossing of the Channel.

Yet for ten miles all was well. Then, just after a huge whale had passed in front of him, his arm gave out. The situation looked hopeless and the British manager, thinking that not even Morgan could swim over a dozen miles through shark-infested waters with only one arm, ordered him to retire. Morgan refused. He would sooner sink than give up and as he trod water by his boat he declared that he fully intended to carry on.

And so, remarkably, he did. With his left arm trailing uselessly by his side, he swam on for another 13 miles until he reached the shore. When he clambered exhausted up the beach the Americans could scarcely believe it. Morgan, operating on only half power, had become the first Englishman to swim the Catalina Straits. This courageous, not to say foolhardy, display won him the Observer Sports Nut of the Year award for 1984.

Wooley Morris A young athlete who broke the ten mile running record but never lived to enjoy it. Attempting to beat the existing mark of 55 minutes, he ran so hard round Richmond Green, Surrey on 15 May 1753 that he not only set a new best time of 54½ minutes but burst a blood vessel and died within the hour. By the time some of the outlying spectators had reached him to offer their congratulations, the new record holder was already a posthumous one.

Captain Gerald Moxom Wedding or no wedding, this gentleman golfer was determined to play in his club's Captain's Prize competition one Saturday in April 1934. So, after graciously consenting to attend the ceremony and re-ception in Bournemouth, he dashed by car to the West Hill Golf Club near Woking, 80 miles away. There, in the fading light and still dressed in his morning suit, he went round in 65 minutes and won the event with a net 71.

John F. Murphy The sad case of an American who fell victim to the pressures of playing golf with the boss. Eager to impress his business associates at the US Carpet Trade Association's annual competition in July 1916, he unfortunately became rather overawed by the occasion. The result, despite a surprisingly economical ten at the last, was a round of 298.

Jack Mytton (1796–1834) Shropshire squire and one of the great sporting lunatics of the nineteenth century. He frittered away a fortune on the horses, drank himself silly, went hunting without any clothes on and terrorised his friends with outrageous practical jokes. The electors of Shrewsbury, who knew good House of Commons material when they saw it, made him their MP but he took no notice. He carried on pleasuring himself to the end of his days, without ever once stopping to count the cost.

Mytton was born on the last day of September 1796 and his eventful youth rather set the tone for the rest of his life. By the age of ten he had his own pack of hounds and his schooldays ended abruptly when he had the distinction of being expelled from both Westminster and Harrow (in his book a sort of scholastic double first). His despairing parents then engaged a private tutor but the young Mytton responded by beating him up. After such a shameful academic career there was really only one place he was fit for: Oxford. He refused to go at first but relented on condition that he read no books save for *The Racing Calendar* and *The Stud Book*.

Three years later he emerged from university a fully qualified hedonist and he could not wait to put his newly acquired knowledge of the Turf to the test. When his father died shortly afterwards, leaving him £60,000 in cash and £10,000 a year, he was suddenly presented with the means to do it. Jack Mytton went to the races in spectacular style and in the course of the next dozen or so years lost a vast fortune breeding and owning racehorses.

Gambling was another of his little weaknesses. At times he seemed merely the middle man through which his legacy passed on its way from the bank vaults to the bookies' pockets. His talent for losing money was outstanding and even if he won he could not seem to hang onto the money for very long. Once, after a rare successful day at Doncaster, he began counting the proceeds in his carriage on the way home. But he fell into a drunken stupor and the winnings, hundreds of pounds all in notes, blew out of the carriage window. When he awoke he did not think it worth the effort to turn the vehicle round and look for the scattered notes.

That was typical of Mytton. He cared for nothing and firmly believed that if there was no risk, there was no point. He was said to have fallen from horses more often than any man alive, hunted naked for duck over a frozen pond, turned over gigs with alarming regularity and was always ready for a fight. On one occasion he was out hunting when a Welsh miner yelled abuse as he rode by. He challenged the burly collier to 20 rounds 'under gentleman's rules', beat him and then sportingly awarded him 10 shillings for his trouble. He fought dogs as well as humans and swore that the best way to do so was to copy the animal's own tactics and use his teeth. Biting them on the nose was apparently particularly effective and he saw off several hounds in this way.

Although wrestling in the street with mongrels was a strange way to show it, he did have a genuine love of animals. He had such respect for the horse that he named one of his children Euphrates after a thoroughbred he owned and none of his regular mounts ever suffered a lack of creature comforts. If, for instance, he was out hunting in cold weather he would always make a point of riding up to a cottage, battering on the door and insisting that both he and his horse were warmed by the labourer's homely fire. Yet some acts of kindness to his dumb friends were not always so successful. Once he gave a bottle of mulled port to a horse called Sportsman and the animal gratefully drained every last drop, then keeled over stone dead. A monkey of his fared better, swallowing in its lifetime lavish quantities of booze with no ill effect whatsoever and frequently accompanying Mytton on his hunting escapades, mounted on its own horse.

Other beasts adapted more slowly to life at Halston Hall. A bear, for example, was prepared to tolerate being ridden into the drawing room while Mytton was mounted on it in full hunting gear, but it drew the line at being pricked with the rider's spurs and bit the squire severely on the leg. The bear was, however, a useful accomplice in Mytton's practical joking and was once put in the bed of one of his more drunken house guests. It was said that the drinker never fully recovered from the shock. His friends would spend an entire stay in dread of such pranks and could not believe their luck when none came. Having spent their visit like coiled springs they then relaxed on the way home, only to be held up by a gruff highwayman. It was Mytton, of course.

It was often difficult to tell if he was joking, or mad or just plain drunk. Frequently it was the latter. After the age of 25 he drank seven bottles of port a day, each glassful topped up with eau-de-cologne, and he loved brandy. The sportsman was not, however, a fussy drinker and once, when a vicious thirst gripped him in a barber's shop, he reached for the lavender water and drank the bottle dry. Clothes, too, were another obsession and at its absurd height his wardrobe was conservatively estimated at 152 pairs of trousers, 152 overcoats, 700 pairs of boots, 1,000 hats and 3,000 shirts.

Keeping Mytton in the mad manner to which he had become accustomed took its toll. In the last 15 years of his life he ripped through over £500,000 and in the end had to sell his estate with all its effects to clear some of his bills. In 1831 he moved into a small hotel in Richmond, then spent the next two years shuttling between Paris and debtors' prison in England. The end came not long after he tried to cure a bout of hiccups by setting fire to his nightshirt. He was badly burned and was never the same again. At last, in March 1834 when life had ceased to be fun, Mytton died aged 37. He was mad, a drunkard and debt-ridden but his sporting antics had given so much pleasure to so many people that there were over 3,000 people at his funeral.

N

Netherton United This poverty-stricken amateur football club in Nottinghamshire were desperate to find the money to keep going. So in 1982, having exhausted all other possibilities, they appealed for cash to the International Monetary Fund. The IMF were more used to bailing governments out of a crisis and said they could not help a private institution but officials there had a whip-round and sent a cheque for £25.

Mike Newton In a few short years this extraordinary specimen transformed himself from a 13 stone fat man into one of the greatest long-distance runners of modern times. He became so devoted to running that even now, in his forties, he covers anything up to 100 miles a day in training and spends every available penny on competing in endurance races the world over.

But back in 1972 that was a future that could never have been imagined. His body then was a monument to the soft life: overweight with a double chin and pot belly. The most arduous exercise he ever took was to wobble down the road to the betting shop or off-licence, and he might have gone on like that had it not been for a suit he owned. It was his favourite suit and when one day he could no longer force his over-flowing flesh into its bursting cloth, he decided that something must be done. And so he started running.

At first, for the want of anything more suitable, he wore his old cricket gear and clattered around the streets near his South London home in flannelled whites and studded boots. But the more he ran the more he liked it. The flannels were replaced by vest and shorts, the double chin and pot belly disappeared and soon there was no stopping him. His training runs took him further and further across the Home Counties and he began to discover that at the distance other athletes were dropping out he was only just getting into his stride. He came to regard the marathon as something of a sprint and started to look for more gruelling challenges. In 1976 he thought he had found it: a 40 mile race at an Epsom track and he duly won it in 4 hours 4 minutes. But he still did not feel as if his remarkable legs had been stretched. Something still longer was needed.

So, just four years after setting out to run some weight off, he joined the small but burgeoning world of ultra-marathon, where strange men run day and night at obscure tracks all over Europe. Always paying and making his own way, he entered every race he could find – a 24 hour event here, a 48 hour race there and 100 kilometre runs seemingly everywhere. His times and distances were a wonder: a new world record for 200 km in 16 hours 40 minutes, 158 miles in 24 hours and 227 miles in 48 hours. But still he always seemed to finish with something in reserve.

Finally in 1981 he heard about the perfect event – the Nottingham Six Day Race. Most people would want to be paid handsomely for spending nearly a full week running but Newton was so keen to take part that he was prepared to pay out of his own pocket for the privilege. So he handed over his £75 and started. For 14 hours, minus a few breaks, he ran round and round the Harvey Hadden stadium until at the finish he had completed 505 miles, won the race and set a new modern world record for the event. In tribute the *Observer* newspaper made him their very first Sports Nut of the Year.

Since then Newton has more than justified the accolade. On the track he has run countless round-the-clock races and on the road he has met innumerable challenges like his Glasgow to Plymouth run in 1983. He has twice competed in the intimidating Athens to Sparta race, each time completing the 158 mile cross-country course in just over a day. The rewards are so slender and the costs so high that he still needs his job as a security officer. He works at night, trains by day and sleeps when he can. The former 13 stone layabout says he has never been happier – proof positive that inside every miserable fat man there is a jolly, thin athlete struggling to get out.

Shuhei Nishida and Sueo Oe A pair of honourable Japanese athletes whose method of settling their sporting differences was fairness itself. They had competed in the pole vault at the 1936 Berlin Olympics and both achieved a height of 13 foot 11¼ inches, which put them level in second place behind gold medallist Earle Meadows. Declining a vault-off to break the tie, they decided that Nishida should be nominally awarded the silver and Oe the bronze and on their return home they would hold a special match to determine who kept which medal.

But back in Japan, even after repeated attempts, the two athletes still cleared the same height. There was only one thing for it, they agreed. They would share the medals – and when Nishida and Oe said share, they meant it quite literally. They went to a jeweller, ordered him to chop their coveted prizes right down the middle and then told him to strike them as unique half-silver, half-bronze Olympic medals.

Richard Milhouse Nixon The 37th President of the United States but the first one ever to change his plans because of a basketball match. In May 1970 there was an air of crisis in the White House. US troops had just invaded Cambodia and four anti-war demonstrators lay dead, shot by the National Guard. But Nixon delayed his televised address to the nation by an hour so as to avoid clashing with the broadcast of the final basketball game between the New York Knickerbockers and the Los Angeles Lakers.

It was no empty or opportunist gesture. In between running America, bothering the world and discussing his latest piece of nefarious business with his henchmen, Nixon always tried to take time out for sport. Gridiron football was a special obsession. Even in the darkest days in his Oval Office bunker, Nixon would spend time working out complicated and devious plays and then ringing coaches to pass on his latest tactical masterpiece.

His nickname of 'Tricky Dicky' did not, however, originate on the football field. At Whittier College between 1930 and 1934 he spent most of the sports sessions sitting on the bench as a reserve tackle. When he did get on the field he was, according to a former team-mate, so eager to get involved that he was invariably off-side. His coach was more generous, recalling that Nixon and his enthusiasm were 'wonderful for morale'. Forty years on, his effect on his fellow countrymen was less inspiring and in 1973 he resigned office to avoid impeachment.

Victor Notaro For a few weeks in the spring of 1981 this young soccer player was the toast of Canada. Playing brilliantly throughout, he had led his country's side to an astonishing victory in a youth World Cup tournament in Australia. Back home the local paper had trumpeted Victor's success on its front page and soon national papers, TV and radio had joined in the excitement. Canada had triumphed, its young players were world champions and Victor was a superstar.

Sad to say he was also a liar. For not only was there no Canadian youth soccer team but there was also no such tournament and Victor had never even left

North America. The football-mad teenager had been so desperate to win his town's 'Sportsman of the Year' title that he had invented the entire event and sent his local paper 'reports' of his starring role in it.

No one could ever accuse Victor of not preparing the ground properly. More than a year before the 'tournament' he had begun sending information about it to newspaper editor Wayne Redshaw. The bulletins came from Kalamazoo, Michigan where Victor was at university on a soccer scholarship. As the February event drew near the reports of Canada's promising squad came thick and fast and were dutifully carried in Redshaw's paper, the *Welland Tribune*. Then came the great kick-off in Australia and the *Tribune*'s readers thrilled to read of the Canadian underdogs' remarkable progress. What was more, the star of the whole show was none other than their own correspondent, Victor Notaro.

He had, of course, been careful not to get the folks back in Welland too excited too early and credited himself with only helping to lay on the goal that beat mighty West Germany in the first round. But there was plenty for them to cheer about in the next round when their own Notaro scored one of the three goals by which Canada beat Brazil. Thus to the final against the feared Soviet Union and who should step up to break the tense, goal-less deadlock but the Welland wizard himself. The *Trib* gave the story full treatment and Mr Redshaw spread the word to the national media. But soon after they took up the story, and with Victor still 'abroad', the truth came out.

He returned to quite a reception. It was not, however, the one that he had been expecting. In place of the parades, the banners and the band there were just Mr Redshaw and Victor's parents. Since they had last seen him he had come quite a long way – 'Australia', 'World Cup star' and now, it seemed, international confidence trickster. The reunion was, as one might imagine, an emotional occasion. Mr Redshaw wanted to know about the fictitious reports he had been sent, Mr and Mrs Notaro wanted to know about what their son thought he was up to and Victor wanted to know if there was a way out of this mess. There wasn't, he duly owned up and someone else was Welland's Sportsman of the Year.

O

Oakland Rugby Club An amateur rugby team in Pittsburgh whose method of intimidating opponents was judged to be so tasteless that they were all banned for life. What they did was to roll human skulls onto the field at Huntingdon, Pennsylvania in an attempt to give the lads for Juniata College the willies. Not surprisingly Juniata objected, as did the University of Pittsburgh Dental School when they discovered where the skulls had come from.

Following the match in March 1982, American rugby officials met to discuss the affair. The punishment they handed out was fairly comprehensive: those involved were suspended for life from playing, officiating, participating, coaching or being an active or inactive member of any rugby football club in the United States.

The rugby administrators were evidently tougher than those in gridiron football. When faced with a worse misdemeanour by a Florida high school coach in 1977 they had merely let him off with a warning. He had apparently tried in his pre-game talks to inculcate aggression into his squad by biting the heads off frogs.

Sir Timothy O'Brien (1861–1948) Middlesex and England batsman who was so keen to preserve his freedom of movement at the crease that he always refused to wear a protective box. Despite such recklessness he managed to remain intact and sired no fewer than 10 children.

Dr Herbert Odom This boxer from Chicago felt it was never too late to turn professional. So on 20 July 1979, at the age of 46 he finally took the plunge.

Fighting as a welterweight he became the oldest man ever to make his paid debut when he took on Eddie Partee, a mere child of 19. It was 23 years since Odom had retired from the amateur ring but in spite of this and the 27 years he was conceding to his opponent, he won in the second round.

Lewis O'Hara An assistant surgeon in the 11th Regiment of Foot who died in defence of his cricketing principles. During a match at Maldon in Essex he began disputing some of the finer points of the game with an Ensign P. Mahon. So implacable did the two sides become that they decided to settle the issue with a duel. O'Hara played and missed but Mahon holed out in the assistant surgeon's head.

Canon A. Wellesley Orr This enterprising parson made valiant efforts between the wars to appeal to the sporting heathen by holding regular 'Football Services'. His church, St Paul's, Kingston Hill, was suitably decked out with corner flags and posts standing in the aisle, players' shirts draped on the pews and miniature goal-posts hanging on the walls. He even opened his sermon with a brief blast on a referee's whistle. Mercifully, he stopped short of dribbling the communion chalice up the aisle or performing sliding tackles on his curate.

George Osbaldeston (1786–1866) The greatest sports nut who ever lived. Throughout his life he devoted every waking hour to play and was never known to buck a challenge. He performed one of the greatest feats in equestrian history by riding 200 miles inside nine hours, once went racing and played billiards for three days and nights without rest, beat the reigning tennis champion with only his gloved hand and even won a cricket match at Lord's with a broken shoulder. As if that was not enough, he was still winning rowing races in his forties, was the best shot and huntsman of his generation, spent his entire fortune on racehorses and frequently risked imprisonment to referee prizefights.

The maniac who accomplished all this and much more was born in London on Boxing Day 1786. If education is meant to be a preparation for the life that follows then Osbaldeston's was perfect. At Eton he forged letters from relatives to obtain 'sham leave' to go shooting and fishing, played hookey to go to Ascot races, often running all the way there and back to avoid detection, and in between attending the odd lesson, excelled at boxing, rowing, cricket and athletics. As he confessed in his autobiography, he did not lead such a reckless career at Oxford where he buckled down and contented himself with rowing, drunken sprees and hunting three times a week.

Shortly after leaving university he inherited the family estates in Yorkshire

GEORGE OSBALDESTON

The greatest sports nut of all time

and so acquired the means for a life of unbridled pleasure. The new squire of Hutton Buscell was not slow to take advantage. He rode, cricketed, hunted, raced, shot, boxed, coursed and rowed with such abandon and to such effect that soon he became known as the Squire of England.

This grand title was bestowed on a very small man. Osbaldeston stood a mere five foot six inches tall and weighed less than 11 stone but what he lacked in size he made up in pugnacity. In boxing matches, like the one against a towering guardsman called Shaw, he would often concede four stone to his opponent and still win. Neither was he afraid of any man's reputation. When J. Edmund Barre, the great real tennis player from France, came to England, Osbaldeston issued an outrageous challenge – his glove against the Frenchman's racket over five sets. He beat him 4-1 and even though his hand was so swollen that he could not use it for a fortnight, he later dared Italian champion Marchasio to meet him on the same terms. Naturally he won that match as well.

What added to the Continentals' ignominy was that Osbaldeston never took tennis very seriously. Cricket was more his game and in his prime he was one of the six best amateurs in the land. He scored centuries for the MCC, Sussex and Epsom, took ten wickets in an innings and claimed he could bowl a ball from one end of Lord's to the other. His speciality was the single and double wicket matches that gentlemen then played for alarmingly high wagers. These were deadly serious affairs and, as the squire once demonstrated, no place for the squeamish.

He was playing with Lord Frederick Beauclerc and Mr E. H. Budd against the three best professionals of the time and at the end of the first day found that his arm was stiff and painful. The agony was such that even the dedicated Osbaldeston declined to bowl any further. But Lord Frederick insisted, plied him with sherry until he was quite drunk and sent him on. He took the ball and in just eight deliveries, dismissed the last professional and won the match. When he had been borne in triumph from the pitch, a surgeon examined him and discovered the cause of his discomfort – a bone in his shoulder was broken.

In other respects Osbaldeston was a sensitive player. Once when he lost a match at Lord's the crowd baited him so much that in a fit of pique he took a pen, scratched out his name from the MCC membership list and rode off, never to return. But what really sealed his fate as a cricketer was the terrible injury he received in a riding accident in 1821. He was hunting with the Atherstone when he collided with another rider, fell and his horse landed on top of him. The result was a double fracture of the right leg so severe that it kept him on his back for two months and left him with a permanent and distressing limp. To most men the injury would have marked the end of an active life but Osbaldeston was different. If anything he rode even more of the mad, cross-country steeplechase races to which he was so addicted. He was so fast that he was never beaten.

Then in 1831, at the age of 45 and still badly incapacitated by his accident, he rode the greatest race of his life. Like so many of his exploits it was prompted by a bet. The wager, with the aptly named General Charritie, was 1,000 guineas to ride 200 miles inside ten hours. The venue was fixed for Newmarket on 5 November and in the preceding weeks he trained like a man possessed, riding 80 miles a day at speed. By the great day he was prepared, as were the 27 thoroughbreds he would ride in relay over the course. Dressed in his purple silks, black velvet cap and deerskin breeches, he was helped into the saddle of his favourite mare Emma and at 12 minutes past seven on a stormy Saturday, he was off. Riding each horse around a circular course for four miles, and some several times, he made the first 100 miles in 4 hours 19 minutes and the entire distance in 8 hours 42 minutes. He had finished with over an hour and a quarter to spare.

It was a great triumph but even then there were those who sneered and to them, indeed to anyone, he flung down this challenge, 'To any man in the world, of any age, weighing or carrying any weight, to ride any distance he prefers from 200 to 500 miles for £20,000.' It was never taken up.

The famous ride signalled his entry onto the Turf. In the end the sport was to cost him some £300,000 but to him it was all money well spent. He rode in every Classic, won races up and down the land and owned Sorella, winner of the One Thousand Guineas in 1844. His gambling involved the inevitable disputes and he took these matters so seriously that he fought two duels over them. But the man who was deadly enough with duelling pistols to once put ten shots on the ace of diamonds at 60 feet, was after satisfaction and not revenge. In the first duel he put his shot through John Gully's hat and in the second Lord George Bentinck fired first and missed, whereupon Osbaldeston aimed deliberately wide. It was a generous act by a man who considered himself poorly used by his lordship's refusal to settle a debt graciously.

But if there was one thing he could abide less than a bad loser, it was anyone who tried to interfere with his sport. Once when 4,000 rioting shoemakers threatened to bring racing to a halt at the Northampton Spring meeting, Osbaldeston, armed only with a blackthorn stick, led five fellow enthusiasts in a charge and dispersed the mob. The meeting continued.

If he would not allow several thousand angry cobblers to stand between him and the 4.15 race, he was certainly not going to allow anything as trivial as the laws of England stop him enjoying a good punch-up. Prizefighting may then have been illegal but it was also good fun and that for the Squire was reason enough to get involved. He refereed dozens of fights, the most notable of them being the 1845 title bout between Bendigo and Caunt in a field near Newport Pagnell. He gave the verdict to Bendigo in the 93rd.

The risk he took to officiate at these illicit gatherings was considerable. In June 1830 he refereed a fight in which the Scottish champion Alexander Mackay lost his life. Arrests were made and a spell in chokey looked distinctly on the cards for Osbaldeston. Luckily he knew what to do. A timely gift of £200 to the magistrate, an accommodating clergyman, and his liberty and good name were preserved.

Boxing had one great virtue which appealed hugely to the Squire and his kind: it involved blood. So did hunting and for most of his life it was one of his particular passions. No fox, hare or gamebird was safe while Osbaldeston was on the loose. He was master of eight hunts and at his peak was riding to hounds six days a week, spending up to 11½ hours in the saddle at a time. As a marksman he had few equals. The pleasure for him was to make the shooting as difficult as possible and he was a leading light in the Old Hats Pigeon Club whose members were sworn to hold their guns under their elbows until the bird was on the wing. Despite this apparent handicap he was capable of wreaking the most awful carnage. He once killed 100 pheasants with 100 shots and in a tour of Scotland bagged 97 grouse with 97 shots, twice despatching two birds with one barrel.

Of course, the life of a country squire was not all fun and games and maiming wildlife. A man in his position had responsibilities and public duties to perform. Chief among these, at the time of the Napoleonic Wars and civil unrest, was the military and in 1809 the 5th Regiment of the North Riding Local Militia made the mistake of appointing him their Lieutenant-Colonel. He lasted less than two years and it is safe to say that he is the only officer in British military history to be reprimanded in front of his men for organising sack races and the like instead of drill practice.

A man in Osbaldeston's class was also expected to put up for Parliament and with great reluctance he agreed the stand for East Retford. He was not, however, prepared for the electors there consuming any of his time or attention beyond polling day. He never once addressed the House of Commons and only visited the place when his sporting engagements permitted.

Advancing age made no difference to him. In his mid-forties he rowed several lengthy races on the Thames and in his fifties was a vigorous competitor in some near-suicidal trotting and coach-driving races, a few of which involved Ben Hur-style events around London squares. Even in his sixties he regarded sleep as time wasted and felt it best to dispense with it. Hence his extraordinary behaviour at the Newmarket Autumn meeting in 1853 when for three days solid he followed the same happy routine: at the races all day, at the billiard table all night, with no rest, no sleep and meals only when strictly necessary. He was 66 at the time and still riding winners. He did not take his last mount until the Goodwood meeting of 1855 when he was 68 and even then he only lost by a neck.

As one would guess, domesticity was always rather an also-ran in Osbaldeston's life and he was unable to spare the time to get married until he was 65. By then, with his estates already sold off to meet his debts, his faculties as well as his means were waning. He spent his last active years watching his few remaining horses run and moving to ever smaller properties in Dorset, Wiltshire, Sussex and London. His circumstances were now considerably reduced and his greatest pleasure was the ritual of each evening when his wife would give him a sovereign pocket-money and he would take a cab to the Portland Club and gamble the coin away at billiards.

Eventually, just before he died on 1 August 1866, Osbaldeston was not even able to go to his club. Incapacitated with gout, the man whom writer Pierce Egan had called 'The Atlas of The Sporting World' was confined to quarters. But he was incorrigible to the last. There was still fun to be had even in his condition and he took a sovereign off a man who wagered him that he could not sit for 24 hours without moving. It was typical of the old Squire. The man who had out-shot, out-rode and out-played his generation could even win a bet in a bath-chair.

William Oscroft This Nottinghamshire opening batsman was having a whale of a time as he started his innings against Yorkshire on 1 June 1875. So much so that when he was suddenly and controversially given run-out, he stubbornly refused to accept the decision. After exchanging a few sharp words with the umpire and wicket-keeper, he and his partner F. Wyld left the field and disappeared into the pavilion. When it was apparent that no Notts batsmen were coming out to replace them, the Yorkshire players and the umpires trooped off as well.

A rather acrimonious meeting then followed, with both Oscroft and the umpires – a wonderful pair called Coward and Luck – adamant that they were right and refusing to budge. Meanwhile the Sheffield crowd, fed up with gazing at an empty field, spilled onto it and began demonstrating for a resumption. At long last Oscroft was persuaded to give up his innings and the match continued. Notts were so impressed with his dogged persistence in the matter that far from disciplining him they later appointed him county captain.

Stan Oxley A chivalrous fast bowler of the 1930s. When taking his fiancée on a blackberrying trip in the country this Malden Wanderers player was so afraid his baser instincts would overwhelm him that he wore his cricket box to ensure his feelings were sufficiently contained. By all accounts the box, to his considerable discomfort, did the trick.

P

Miss Dorothy Paget This wealthy racehorse owner was haunted by a pathological fear that she might not arrive at the races on time. Her phobia dated from a horrible experience she once had when her car broke down and she missed an entire meeting. She vowed that this calamity should never happen again. So from then on, whenever Miss Paget set off for the racecourse in her limousine, her second chauffeur followed behind in a spare car.

It was not her only eccentricity. She had a strong aversion to men, particularly their smell according to Lord Porchester, habitually wore a shabby old coat to the races, gambled furiously and was a terrible old night bird, ringing trainers at all hours to discuss prospects. But slightly touched she may have been, silly she was not. She owned the great Golden Miller who won the Grand National and five Cheltenham Gold Cups and in 1943 was the leading owner on the Flat.

Eduardo Angel Pazos A courageous football official, he refused to be intimidated by the partisan home crowd when refereeing the Peru v Argentina match in 1964. With just two minutes to go the Peruvians equalized and their supporters went crazy with delight. Until, that is, Pazos disallowed the goal and then they just went crazy. His decision sparked off a mass riot which left 301 dead, over 500 injured and every window in the Lima stadium broken. Afterwards, with tear gas still wafting over the ground, Pazos was pressed for a comment on his decision. 'Maybe it was a goal,' he said, 'anyone can make a mistake.'

Mr Pedrick For centuries the human race has been plagued with the problem of how to keep a golf ball on the straight and narrow. Often even the thought of yet another shot careering wildly off the line has been enough to make grown men weep, calm ones break down and strong, silent types be reduced to gibbering wrecks. But this English inventor was determined to end their suffering. At last in 1967, after months of calculations and experiment, Mr Pedrick unveiled his solution: a golf ball with wings.

The device he patented consisted of a ball fitted with hinged flaps which flew out when the ball started to spin in the air. The idea was that these wings would steady the ball's flight. As Mr Pedrick modestly said at the time, 'If this can be achieved considerable benefit will have been added to the general happiness of mankind.' Unfortunately the boffin appeared to know more about aerodynamics than he did about the rules of golf, for his ball was completely illegal and never got off the ground.

Bobby Peel (1857–1941) One of the greatest boozers ever to appear on a sports field. As a cricketer for Yorkshire and England he may have been good enough to take 100 wickets in a season nine times and score a double century but as a drinker he was better than that, indisputably world class. He sometimes arrived at matches very much the worse for wear and once he had made his weaving way to the middle would stand there wondering where he was and what he was supposed to be doing.

Except on extreme occasions, the alcoholic haze through which he bowled had no effect whatsoever on his performance. Indeed there were times, like the 1894 Sydney Test, when it actually seemed to improve his game. Here the England captain Andrew Stoddart had to put Peel under a shower to sober up before he was steady enough on his feet to go out for the final day's play. With a muzzy head and a bleary eye he then proceeded to demolish the Australian batting by taking six wickets for 67 runs.

Inevitably the day had to come when there was no friendly skipper to pull him round and his career came to a celebrated and fitting climax in a match at Sheffield in 1897. Still pie-eyed from the night before, he reeled onto the pitch, took the ball, ran the wrong way and, to general amazement, bowled it at the pavilion. Then, by way of an encore, he relieved himself on the pitch. It was all to much for Lord Hawke, Yorkshire's aristocratic captain, and he ordered Peel from the field and told him never to darken the team's dressing room again.

David Francis Long Pentecost The angler who was so desperate that he even tried fishing in his town's main drainage system. But the only thing he landed was an appearance in court. A policeman on patrol in Rochdale had come across Pentecost sitting on the pavement with his line dangling down a drain grating. After his arrest for obstruction he told the court, 'I am fighting for the right of anyone to fish where they like.' He was fined £5.

Peter (1950–1964) This cat loved cricket so much that he adopted Lord's as his home territory and spent the rest of his life watching matches there. Often, when the game had reached a particularly absorbing point, his sleek, black figure could be seen prowling onto the pitch to observe proceedings at closer range. Eventually, after 12 years' residence at cricket's headquarters, he passed away and became the first cat to have his obituary appear in *Wisden*. The eulogy even included a solemn tribute from the secretary of the MCC, Mr Billy Griffith.

Walter Poenisch Snr. A 64-year-old American, he just loved going for a dip in the sea and as far as he was concerned the further he went the better. But one day in 1978 he excelled himself. Setting off from Havana, Cuba on 13 July he struck out across the Florida Straits with no intention of stopping until he had reached the United States. Swimming inside a shark cage and pulled along by helpful tides, he landed at Little Duck Key, Florida just 34 hours and 15 minutes later. It was an absurd performance. The old man had crossed 128 miles of seas and so achieved, by many a stroke, the longest ocean swim in history.

Raymond Priestley Snooker may not seem to be a very dangerous game but it was the way this Australian played it. He was having a few frames with a friend in his Melbourne garage one day when the white rolled into an awkward position. It was his shot but no matter how he arranged himself in the garage's confined space, there was no way that he could play the cue ball as he wanted. A lesser man might have settled for a simple safety shot, but not Priestley. He knew there was a good chance of a pot, there was just a chance of getting to it.

All at once he saw a way. Climbing onto a chair and then a bench, he swung himself over a crossbeam in the ceiling and hung there upside down by his legs. Cue in hand, all he had to do now to hit the ball was just reach down a bit, extend his arm and stretch a little more and. . . . It was too much. He slipped, crashed onto the concrete floor head first and died later from his injuries.

Edward Pooley (1838–1907) An England cricketer who missed a Test match – all because of a bet. He was a member of the first England touring party to visit New Zealand and while he was there he hatched a plan to supplement his meagre match fees. Just before an up-country game against a local XVIII he

Cricket connoisseur

offered odds of 20-1 in shillings that he could forecast the precise score of each member of the opposition. A man called Donkin thought this sounded like a good thing and he took up the offer. Pooley, however, had made a study of these matters. He predicted a duck for each batsman and when four of them duly failed to score he collected £4 as against a loss of only 14 shillings.

Mr Donkin was not happy. He claimed he had been taken for a mug, which he clearly was, and refused to cough up. A scuffle then ensued and at the end of the next match in Otago, Pooley and the baggage man Bramall were arrested, fined and remanded on a charge of injuring property above the value of £5. So, while the rest of the party went off to Australia to play the world's first two Test matches, Pooley, their regular wicket-keeper, languished in a New Zealand jail. He was eventually brought before the Supreme Court where he was acquitted, much to the relief of the local populace who had always supported him. Indeed, the New Zealanders were so embarrassed at the rough treatment Pooley had received that they had a whip-round and in due course presented the wicket-keeper with £50 and a gold watch as a memento of his adventure.

Q

Duke of Queensbury (1725–1810) William Wordsworth called him degenerate and his rivals on the Turf said he was unscrupulous, but no one could ever have accused this aristocrat of not taking his sport seriously. The reason was that everything he did as a cricketer, jockey or racehorse owner was accompanied by a large bet, always obtained at the most favourable of odds. He was one of the most cunning old devils with a wager that ever was and when he died he left over £1 million.

Most of these ill-gotten gains were acquired through some fairly nifty coups on the racecourse but if he thought there was a profit in it he would have a flutter on anything. When he was given the honour of captaining an England cricket side against Eton in 1751 he could not resist wagering £1,500 on the outcome and the health of a friend was always worth the risk of a few 'sovs', as were some of the period's more disgusting eating contests. One shudders to think of what had to be shovelled away before Queensbury's man beat Sir John Lade's candidate 'by a pig and an apple pie' in 1759.

In all his gambling he was as crafty as a monkey. Once he was bet that he could not send a message 50 miles within an hour and he won by having the note sewn inside a ball which was then hurled from man to man by 24 cricketers standing in a wide circle. There was, he explained to his furious victim, nothing in the rules to say that the message had to travel in a straight line. On another occasion, when he was 35, he took a sizeable sum from the Irish punter Count Theobald O'Taffe by winning a wager that a horse and carriage could not travel at 19 miles an hour. The Count was probably right, an ordinary contraption could not go at that speed. But the carriage which the conniving Queensbury put onto Newmarket Heath was anything but ordinary, being made out of thin wood and whalebone and fitted with silken harnesses. It performed the feat with six and a half minutes to spare.

Throughout his life he was served by an uncanny instinct for protecting his money and saving his skin. He could smell trouble as if it were a sickly perfume. At Newmarket in 1756 he somehow got wind of a bribe that had been paid to his jockey. Just before the 'off' he marched up to the start, threw off a cloak beneath which he was dressed in his own scarlet racing colours, rode the horse himself and won. Another time, after a particularly acrimonious challenge race at The Curragh in Ireland, his opponent Sir Ralph Gore appeared on the course itching for a duel and so confident of success that he brought with him an oak coffin bearing Queensbury's coat of arms and the current date. The prudent old Duke took one look at the bier, apologised and vanished. He invariably knew when to back and when to back off.

Indeed he never took the slightest chance with his health. It was just as well, for he gave his body a fearful bashing with over half a century of incessant philandering. He was a member of the notorious Hell Fire Club, a sort of rake's MCC, and in his old age he would sit on the balcony of his Piccadilly home spying likely-looking talent whom his staff would then try to procure. Sticking to young girls, rather than the raddled and diseased harridans usually on offer to his kind, was part of the secret of his health and vigour. So too was his almost total abstinence from alcohol, belief in a good night's sleep and moderate eating habits. As he grew older his concern for fitness became raging hypochondria and he not only spent vast sums on patent remedies but engaged a French physician who was paid for every day that he kept his master alive.

Despite all these precautions he eventually began to show marked signs of wear and tear and in 1810 it became apparent that the end was drawing near. Inspired by this, some cronies opened a book on his death and Queensbury was tempted by the odds to risk £500 himself by betting that he would be dead by a certain day in November. How he had ever expected to collect had he been proved right remains a mystery. But his guess was wrong, the day passed, he had to pay out and he actually died a month later. It was probably the thought of losing this bet that finally killed the old gambler off.

R

Floyd Reed This American golfer felt rather hemmed in on the average course. What he needed was something that gave him a bit more scope. So in 1963 he devised and played the longest hole in the world – 5,978,720 yards long, stretching from coast to coast right across America. He teed off on the Pacific shore in California in late June and finally finished a year and 114 days later with a deft chip into the Atlantic. In between he had covered 3,397 miles, played 114,737 shots, incurred 3,511 self-imposed penalty strokes and lost countless balls.

Richmond Golf Club It was 1940, in the dark days of the Second World War and England stood alone. Up in the air the Battle of Britain was raging, Spitfires were locked in mortal combat with Messerschmitts and the skies were thick with the smoke and sounds of conflict. But down on the ground the members of Richmond Golf Club in Surrey were trying to get on with a quiet game of golf.

It was not easy. In fact at times the inconsiderate action of the Luftwaffe, 15,000 feet overhead, definitely bodged up a damn fine game. Sometimes a chap might be about to play when a burst of machine gun fire would put him completely off his stroke – or he might see his perfectly-positioned drive blown right out of bounds by half a ton of airborne explosive. It was all dashed difficult.

The club secretary was most concerned about this intrusion into his members' golf. So he devised and issued a set of emergency rules covering every eventuality of war-time golf:

'1. Players are asked to collect bomb and shrapnel splinters to save these causing damage to the mowing machines.

2. In competitions, during gunfire or while bombs are falling, players may take cover without penalty for ceasing play.

3. The position of known delayed-action bombs are marked by red flags at a reasonably, but not guaranteed safe, distance therefrom.

4. Shrapnel and/or bomb splinters on the fairways, or in bunkers within a club's length of a ball, may be moved without penalty and no penalty shall be incurred if a ball is thereby caused to move accidentally.

5. A ball moved by enemy action may be replaced, or if lost or destroyed, the ball may be dropped not nearer the hole without penalty.

6. A ball lying in a crater may be lifted and dropped not nearer the hole, preserving the line to the hole, without penalty.

7. A player whose stroke is affected by the simultaneous explosion of a bomb may play another ball from the same place. Penalty one stroke.'

Thanks to these rules Richmond's small corps of dedicated golfers were able to play on, untroubled and without dispute, for the rest of the duration. Their devotion to sporting duty in the face of enemy action earned them a certain amount of celebrity when reported in the newspapers. Not in Germany, however. When news of the Richmond rules reached the Ministry for Propaganda and Public Enlightenment in Berlin, Dr Joseph Goebbels himself was so incensed that he went on German radio to condemn them.

'By means of these ridiculous reforms,' he spluttered, 'the English snobs try to impress the people with a kind of pretended heroism. They can do so without danger, because as everyone knows, the German Air Force devotes itself only to the destruction of military targets and objectives of importance to the war effort.'

As an attempt at the truth Goebbel's statement was an air shot and Richmond's golfers absorbed his insults every bit as well as all the bombs, incendiaries and land-mines that continued to be hurled in their direction.

Peter Richmond A policeman and rugby referee who solved the problem of enforcing law and order at the Abingdon v Didcot match by getting rid of every player on the field. The game was being played just two days after Christmas 1982 but any festive goodwill there may have been soon evaporated when a punch-up started and the match rapidly degenerated into a general free-for-all. Finally Mr Richmond called the two captains together, said, 'I've had enough, I'm fed up with it,' and sent off all 30 players.

Roy Riegles This gridiron footballer brought a dull game to spectacular life by running almost the length of the field for a touchdown. There was, however, just one small blemish. He had run the wrong way and so scored one of the most galling own goals in sporting history.

Riegles's boob happened at the 1929 Rosebowl game when his side, University of California, faced Georgia Tech. With very little time left California were 7-6 ahead and pressing deep into Georgia territory. As both sides fought desperately for possession there developed an almighty, wheeling scramble out of whose tangle of limbs the ball suddenly popped like a bar of wet soap. Riegles shook himself free, picked up the precious ball and, obviously having lost his bearings in the melee, started off back towards his own side's half.

In the general confusion it took a few seconds for the penny to drop but when it did the Californians in the stands and on the pitch did all they could to stop their runaway lineman. The crowd roared but Riegles just assumed they were cheering him on his way and ran even harder. The Californian backs hared after him but when he heard the thump of pursuing feet he just got his head down and accelerated. He was now but yards from his objective and shaking off a last, lunging tackle from one of his own side, he dived for the end zone and scored.

When his team-mates finally caught up with him they speedily re-acquainted him with the broad geography of the football field. As the awful truth sunk in he realised that his stirring run had given Georgia a somewhat undeserved win.

Minnie Roberts Minnie was decidedly mini. She stood only 4 foot 11 inches tall and weighed in at a mere 8 stone 6 pounds. But that did not stop this 66-year-old grandmother entering and winning a weightlifting contest. She triumphed in the 1984 Michigan State Championship for women over 40 by hoisting almost twice her own bodyweight and can now claim to be probably the strongest little old lady in the world.

Alberto Rodriguez A Portuguese golf enthusiast, he was determined that his son should grow up to be a champion at the game. In order to give eight month old Albertini the best possible start in life he had him baptised in the lake separating tee and green at the par three sixth at Quinta da Lagos. As the protesting infant was dunked in the water hazard one day in 1983, his father solemnly addressed him with these words, 'You have now been in this water once but I never want to hear of you in it again when you play golf.'

Leigh Richmond Roose Doctor, goalkeeper and one of the most outlandish characters ever to stand beneath a crossbar. In a dozen or so seasons before the Great War this Welshman established a reputation for practical joking, superstitions and eccentric play that may never be matched. He refused ever to have his football shirt washed, once fooled the Welsh FA into believing he was irreparably injured and kept goal in an extraordinary fashion for ten different clubs. Yet the amateur was good enough between the posts to play for his country no fewer than 24 times.

Born the son of a Presbyterian Minister in Wrexham, he played his early football for Druids, Northern Nomads and Aberystwyth. Then his medical work took him to London and from then until the end of his career he represented a string of clubs: London Welsh, Stoke, Everton, Sunderland, Huddersfield, Aston Villa and Arsenal. Each was glad to have him but his services could sometimes cost them dear. Living in London he frequently travelled great distances for a game and if the scheduled train did not suit him he would hire a special train and charge the club.

His strange behaviour would thus begin long before he reached the ground. One of his favourite japes at a railway station was to summon a porter to his carriage and ask him if he would be so kind as to feed his dog who was incarcerated in the guard's van. The obliging railwayman would then walk the entire length of the train with his hands full of dog biscuits, only to discover when he got there that there was no dog. Upon his return to protest there would be no Roose either.

Often his chartered train would arrive at its destination only minutes before the kick-off and so the first sight that anxious club officials would have of him would be as he tore up to the ground at the reins of a hansom cab, for which, of course, they would subsequently have to pay. Once inside the dressing room, no matter whose jersey he was about to wear, he would always pull on the same undershirt. He believed it to be unlucky if it was ever washed and so this disgusting garment never once saw the inside of a laundry. It was a strange superstition for a bacteriologist to have.

When he got onto the pitch his shirt was not the only reason why the opposing forwards kept their distance. He was in fact a formidable goalkeeper, able to punch the ball further than most men could kick it and possessed of an uncanny sense of position. This may have been due to the weird ritual he observed at the beginning of each match when he would pace out his goalmouth with great deliberation and care.

During the game Roose was capable of almost anything, making the most breathtaking saves or committing the most atrocious of errors. Neither did the good doctor feel constrained to stay in his goal area if he saw fit. Once, when Wales were reduced to ten men, he refused to hear of a forward being pulled back and insisted on plugging the gap himself by playing at both full-back and in goal – and he duly did so. Of course, if there was nothing to directly engage his attention he would simply sit down by one of the uprights and chat to the crowd.

Yet, despite his waywardness, his value to Wales was immense and their dependence on him provided the vehicle for perhaps his finest hoax. They were playing Northern Ireland and Roose thought it would be a good idea to scare the life out of the Welsh officials by turning up for the boat to Belfast with a heavily bandaged hand. 'Not to worry,' he told the rest of the party, knowing that they would, 'it's only a couple of broken bones. I'm sure I can still play.'

As a medical man and experienced cap he was well placed to keep up the act without being challenged and when he appeared the following morning with the bandage still on, the news had spread far and wide that he was going to play with a pair of broken fingers. Some of the shrewder Welshmen had already guessed what he was up to but when Roose ran onto the pitch every photographer in the ground was clustered by his goal to capture the historic appearance of an invalid in an international match. Then, as the whistle blew, he turned to the cameraman, smiled broadly and unwound the bandages to reveal two perfectly sound fingers. Naturally he topped his own gag by playing brilliantly in a Welsh win.

It was one of his last great performances. A few years later the First World War broke out, Roose joined up and he was soon on his way across the Channel to fight in France. Like so many others he did not come back.

Stuart Russell A pool player who became rather too attached to his table. His troubles had begun halfway through a match at the Eagle Inn, Oswestry in Shropshire. He was leaning over the table and about to take aim when he coughed with such violence that two of his false teeth flew out, went straight into the corner pocket and disappeared. Russell was aghast. Those teeth meant a lot to him and in an instant he was round the table thrusting his right arm into the pocket to retrieve them.

But what goes down does not always come up and when he tried to remove his arm he found that it was well and truly stuck. Soon the attention of the Eagle's customers was drawn to this immobolised figure, part of whom appeared to be fixed in some way to their pool table. They came round and tried to free him but his arm just would not budge. The police, who had been summoned, found it a problem too, as did the six firemen when they arrived on the scene.

Eventually, however, the table top was lifted, Russell's arm released and he was re-united with his teeth. He put them back in his mouth, thanked his rescuers, replaced the balls, continued the game and won.

David Ryder In 1969 this polio victim walked the 872 miles from John

O'Groats to Land's End on crutches. It seemed then a literally staggering performance but to Ryder it was just a training session. The next year he crossed America aided once more by crutches – he covered the 2,960 miles in only 106 days.

S

Joe Sallas This American boxer was such a good sport that his biggest defeat was also his greatest victory. He came from California and had started in the fight game as a boy when he joined the local boxing club. His best pal Jackie Fields had started with him and soon the two boys who had grown up together were training side by side and boxing in all the tournaments they could find. They were both featherweights and both good, so good in fact that as they rose to championship level there was little to choose between them. That, however, was not what the American Olympic boxing selectors thought and when they drew up their team for the 1924 Games, Sallas was in and Fields out.

Far from being happy Sallas was very upset and annoyed. He thought his friend should have been chosen and such was his sense of fair play that he was prepared to jeopardise everything – his own place in the team and, if necessary, his entire career – to get the selectors to change their minds. He threatened to withdraw from the squad unless Fields was included and when that didn't work he launched an all-out campaign in favour of his friend, writing to newspapers, pleading with the boxing authorities and bombarding the selectors with letters. Finally they relented. Fields was included in the team and the two chums travelled to Paris to try their luck at the Games.

Having had such a hard fight to get to the Olympics they were certainly not going to waste that effort with a careless moment in the ring. For round after round, bout after bout they boxed brilliantly until, amazingly, they faced each other in the final of the featherweight tournament. When it came to the fight they put their friendship briefly aside and boxed ferociously. After a fearsome fight Fields won. He had beaten the man who had risked everything to bring him to the Olympics. Sallas had been proved right, his best pal was good enough to fight at the Games.

Earl of Sandwich (1718–1792) Aristocrat, fast food inventor and cricket enthusiast. He was so keen on the game that when one day in 1745 he was summoned to a government meeting at the Admiralty, he sent back the message, 'I'll be at your board when at leisure from cricket.' He did not like his indoor sports interrupted either, hence the snack he originated which meant he could play at the gaming tables and eat at the same time.

Hedonism was his other great love and he was said by a fellow-member of the infamous Hell-Fire Club to be as 'lecherous as a goat'. He was also reported to have held burlesque services in a village church where he preached blasphemous sermons to a congregation of cats. Apart from that, fighting the odd duel and seeing one of his mistresses shot dead by a love-crazed clergyman, he was respectability itself.

Michael Scaglione (1956–1982) A short-tempered American golfer who came to a premature and sticky end. He was playing at the City Park West Municipal course, New Orleans in April 1982 when suddenly, at the 13th hole, he duffed an important stroke. He was livid and in his fury hurled the offending club against his golf cart. The clubshaft broke and the head, attached to a few inches of jagged shaft, ricocheted back and stabbed Scaglione in the throat. He fell back and managed to tear the fractured club from his neck. But his jugular was severed and he died later from his injuries, a terrible warning to all those who get mad and throw clubs on the golf course.

William Scotton (1856–1893) Loss of form is seldom fatal but it was for this Nottinghamshire cricketer. He was so depressed at losing his place in the county side that he committed suicide. Thus ended at the age of 38, the life of perhaps the most boring batsman ever to play the first class game. Indeed *Wisden* – never a publication knowingly to kick a cricketer when he is down – said of him on his death, 'He carried caution to such extremes that it was often impossible to take any pleasure in seeing him play.'

His slow scoring performances were legendary. At the 1886 Oval Test he spent 225 minutes over an innings of 34 (going 67 of these interminable minutes without adding a single run) and on another occasion he took 155 minutes to score 17. But in 1890 he excelled himself, inflicting on the paying customers at Gravesend, Kent two hours of blocking and padding for a mere six runs.

These painstaking displays were so dreadful to witness that soon Scotton was even being sent up by *Punch*. In some lines of verse entitled *Wail of the Weary* their resident satirist wrote –

'And the clock's slow hands go round,
And you still keep up your sticks
But, oh, for the lift of a smiting hand
And the sound of a swipe for six.'

It was hardly Swift but it made the point, especially to someone as sensitive as Scotton (a colleague once said of him that he would weep at the slightest provocation). So, with his spirits lowered by public criticism, the shock of being dropped was the final blow. These matters preyed on his mind for some time and then on 9 July 1893, the man who had in his younger days been hailed as one of the best left-handers in England, went back to his lodgings in St John's Wood and killed himself.

Miss Ena Shaw On 23 November 1931 this obliging young lady became The Human Golf Tee. She spent a nerve-wracking few hours on that day laying down at the start of Esher Golf Club's 18 holes and allowing professional George Ashdown to drive from a rubber device strapped to her forehead. Her faith in his swing was well-placed and she emerged unscathed.

Canon Lancelot Smith A resourceful reverend cricketer, he once managed to incorporate the burial of a parishioner into the middle of his innings. The rather disrespectful incident happened during a match against a team of Indian students at Spalding, Lincolnshire in 1926. Canon Smith's side were batting and knowing he had a funeral to conduct in the middle of the day, he was somewhat perturbed to find himself one of the not out batsmen at lunch. As soon as the interval began he hurried from the ground and zipped through the interment service at something in excess of medium pace. He was then able to return from the cemetery in time to walk sedately to the wicket with his pre-lunch partner, not having missed a single ball.

Tony Smith A West Country club cricketer who took to the field just ten minutes after undergoing a two-hour operation in hospital. His act of heroism was prompted by the desperate plight of his side Bristol Clifton in their match against Lansdowne of Bath in 1983. Earlier in the game, when Smith was keeping wicket, a ball had smashed into his teeth and caused such extensive damage that he had to be taken off for surgery at the Bath Royal United Hospital, conveniently sited next to the ground.

But while Smith was under the knife, his team were on the slide. News of their crisis reached him and as soon as the doctors had patched him up he hurried back to the ground where he found his team needing 19 to win in just over three overs. At that moment another wicket fell and Smith, despite his injury, the two-hour operation and the effects of the local anaesthetic, insisted on batting. In the best traditions of such recklessness he then proceeded to score 13 of the vital runs and win the match.

Forrest Smithson An American athlete and theology student, he was so upset at athletics being staged on the Sabbath at the 1908 Olympics that he decided to make a small gesture of protest. When it came to his event, the 110 metres hurdles, he ran the entire race while carrying a Bible in his left hand. Despite his piece of luggage, he not only won the gold medal but also set a new world record of 15.0 seconds.

Gordon Speake and James Stewart When dedicated golfers have their heads down and are hell-bent on their game, they cannot be deflected. Not even, as in the case of these two Hampshire players, when their path is crossed by a trio of escaping prisoners and the forces of law and order in determined pursuit.

The pair were playing their weekly round one day in May 1983 when, unbeknown to them, the great break-out occurred. Six convicts, being transferred by prison coach from Wandsworth jail to Parkhurst on the Isle of Wight, staged a mock fight as the vehicle neared the Surrey-Hants border. In the ensuing melee they pinched the keys, opened the doors and three of them sprang to freedom across Liphook golf course. The prison officers escorting them gave chase and soon a regular hue and cry was in progress all over the fairways.

Enter Mssrs Speake and Stewart, locked in golfing combat. 'Of course, we knew nothing about the escaped convicts at the time,' said Mr Speake afterwards, 'there were a lot of people chasing up the 15th as we were playing down the 16th and we thought it was just an army exercise . . .' That impression was swiftly corrected. As Mr Stewart said, 'Then we saw they were being pursued by a man in uniform. He shouted at us, "For God's sake, phone the police." '

It was a testing moment. What would it be, golf or civic duty? But luck was on their side. 'At that moment,' explained Mr Stewart, 'the postman came round the corner in his van on the way to the clubhouse and we told him to tell the secretary to raise the alarm.' Having thus disposed of the problem, the two sportsmen continued their tense match without further interruption. They were able to finish their game just minutes before the course was closed to allow police dog handlers to swarm onto the links in search of the fugitives. All were finally recaptured.

Springwood Bowls Club This club in Brisbane, Australia had a particularly dedicated member called Max. He played every day whatever the weather. Finally the club agreed to honour this stalwart and at a New Year gathering in 1982 they made him a presentation. It was, however, a somewhat calculated gift, for they gave him life membership and Max was 102 years old.

Lt Alfred Starbird An indomitable American, he was certainly not going to let a broken bone in his foot prevent him competing in the gruelling modern pentathlon at the 1936 Olympics. The fracture came just before the start of the contest but he insisted on having a go at all five events – the shooting, fencing, horse riding, swimming and even the 4,000 metres cross-country race. Immediately after the competition, in which he finished a courageous seventh, he was taken to hospital and the foot put into plaster.

Start F.C. The most heroic football team ever to take the field. They never played in any cups or leagues, never travelled beyond their own city and lasted only a very short while, but this Ukrainian side won perhaps the most inspiring victory in all sport.

It came in the summer of 1942. Hitler's army had settled into their brutal occupation of Russia and among the cities in their grip was Kiev. Before the war the local side, Dynamo, was among the best in the country but when mobilisation began the team's players were drafted into the Red Army. In due course they fought and were taken prisoner. The Germans put most of them to work as porters at No. 1 bakery in Kiev and here they formed a football team which became known as Start.

They did not have to wait long for their first match. The Germans wanted to open up the local stadium again and they chose to do so on 12 June with a match between Start and a German army unit. Much to the annoyance of the German top brass, Start won. Neither was the Nazi temper improved by the next match on 17 July. This time Start beat a far stronger German side – PGS – by the humiliating margin of 6-0. The football reporter for the local German-controlled paper rose to the occasion. 'The fact that our team lost,' he wrote, 'must not be regarded as an achievement on the part of members of the Start team.'

For the next match, on 19 July, the Ukrainians were matched against a

Hungarian team, MSG Wal. They won this 5-1 but in the return a week later Start could only scrape home 3-2. This relatively poor performance was siezed upon by the Germans. They had been infuriated by the partisan feelings that Start's victories had stirred up and when they heard this latest result they felt that the time was now ripe for Start FC to be slapped down. In a matter of days the authorities had fixed a match for them against the crack German army team Flakelf.

It was an intimidating prospect. Flakelf were superbly fit and unbeaten in occupied territory. Start, meanwhile, were not in quite the condition their record may have suggested. Their side may have contained a good nucleus of Dynamo Kiev players but they were in reality a rag-bag assortment ravaged by war. They were half-starved, living in virtual siege conditions and in no real state to play an intense programme of matches. Against Flakelf on 6 August they seemed to be on the original hiding to nothing.

But they had their pride and fired by this they played so well that at half-time they actually led 2-1. The second half would be different, they told themselves. Indeed it was; the Germans did not score at all. Instead Start applied even heavier pressure to the Flakelf goal, scored three more times and ran out 5-1 winners. The Germans were incensed. Their team's proud record, not to mention the reputation of the glorious Third Reich, had been at the mercy of this makeshift team of Ukrainians. Something had to be done.

It was, but it didn't have much to do with sport. As the Ukrainians were still celebrating in their dressing room a Nazi officer was despatched to see them. He told the players that a return game had already been arranged for three days' time. He also reminded them that until Flakelf had met Start they had not lost a match and the indignity of doing so again would not be tolerated. Then, quite coldly, he said, 'If you do not lose the game you will be shot.'

The team listened in stunned silence and when the officer left they were in complete agreement, the Germans meant what they said. The dilemma they faced was clear-cut: lose a game of football or face the firing squad. When they re-assembled at the Zenith Stadium three days later, Start's players knew they really only had one choice. They could not let their own people down. They would go out and beat the Germans as they had never beaten any team before.

From the moment the whistle blew Start were brilliant, dribbling round storm-troopers, junking past infantrymen and totally over-running the defence. In no time at all they had scored. If the Germans thought that this was just Start's small gesture of theatrical defiance before they caved in, they were wrong. The longer the match went on the more obvious it became that Start had no intention of losing. Eventually, with the Ukrainians comfortably ahead and distinct signs of agitation appearing among the German high command in the stands, the referee cut the game short.

It was the signal for the Germans to fulfill their pre-match threat. Before the Start players had even left the pitch they were arrested, bundled into a closed van and taken away to Babi Yar, a ravine to the northeast of Kiev. There, still in the shirts they had worn with such fierce pride, they were lined up and shot. The team that refused to be beaten had died with their boots on.

Bob Steer Sussex soccer fan who preferred to go and see Brighton and Hove Albion play football rather than attend his son's wedding. It was, after all, a very special occasion. His favourite team were playing their very first match in Division One and having witnessed more than a few weddings in his time, the sentimental old so-and-so decided to give the nuptials a miss. His wife Mary supported him. 'This', she said with unconscious irony, 'is a storybook match for him.'

So, while his son Colin married Alison Hill in the other match of that day in August 1977, the 56-year-old British Rail clerk went to his usual seat at the Goldstone ground to see the game against Arsenal. It was not a happy event, Brighton lost 4-0.

Andrew Stoddart (1863–1915) A compulsive all-rounder. He captained England at three different sports (cricket, rugby union and Australian rules football), was a scratch golfer and first class boxer, excelled at tennis, billiards and real tennis, played hockey for Hampstead and for a while was even the secretary for the Neasden Golf Club.

His idea of time well spent was encapsulated by one glorious Wednesday in August 1886. After playing poker all night he left the tables at dawn, freshened up with a swim, breakfasted and then travelled to Hampstead Cricket Club for the match against the Stoics. He went to the wicket at 11.30 and batted with such unrestrained aggression that by lunch the score had reached a ludicrous 370-2. Greater madness was to follow in the afternoon. The man who had not slept for over 30 hours laid into the bowling without a shred of compassion and the scorers were scarcely able to keep up. He rapidly passed the milestones of 200 and 300 runs and at 5 p.m. went roaring beyond 400. It was only the close of play that brought the onslaught to an end; the rattling scoreboard being silenced at last with Stoddart on 485 not out (64 fours and three sixes) and the total on 813.

His day was still far from over. He went directly from the cricket ground to the tennis court, played a tough three-set doubles match, had a bath, took a cab to the theatre, dined afterwards and finally got to bed at 3 a.m. He completed the week's work by making 207 runs in even time on the Saturday and then hitting an innings of 98 for Middlesex on the Monday. In three days of cricket he had scored 790 runs and it seems only fitting that he should have rounded off that season by making 110 with a broomstick.

Such a hectic life left little time for frivolities like marriage and it was not until he was 43 that he was able to accommodate a wedding into his schedule. Sport, however, was never far from his mind and even on the very morning of the nuptials, as his demure bride Ethel Luckham prepared nervously for the afternoon ceremony at St Stephen the Martyr, Stoddart and partner were playing a pre-marital game of golf with the vicar and organist. They lost 2 and 1.

His marriage was a landmark. All his glories were now firmly in the past. Alas he was never able to come to terms with his fading powers and money worries only deepened his depressions. Finally, on Easter Saturday 1915, the once-great sportsman withdrew to a room in his London home and shot himself.

Bram Stoker (1847–1912) Failed athlete who later turned to authorship where his warped mind created *Count Dracula*, a story of almost unrelieved unpleasantness. As a tall, red-bearded young man of 21 he won the 1868 Civil Service Five Mile Walk but was disqualified for lifting (i.e. breaking into a running stride). It was, perhaps, this disappointing experience that turned his imagination towards Transylvania.

R. S. Surtees (1803–1864) The author of the famous 'Jorrocks' stories and something of a sporting hypocrite. He managed to combine a rabid enthusiasm for hunting and the slaughter of wildlife with a deep-seated aversion to boxing. His feelings ran so strong that when he founded and edited a sports magazine he banned any mention of fisticuffs from its pages. He believed it to be 'a low and demoralising pursuit' which should not be encouraged in any way and certainly not by his *New Sporting Magazine*.

Bruce Sutherland A physical education teacher and Scotsman who died from that happily rare condition, an excess of golf. He had wanted to discover how many rounds he could play before he dropped and in 1927 he found out. Starting at 8.15 a.m. on 21 June he began to hit his way round Craiglockhart Links, Edinburgh with hardly a break. He made circuit after circuit of the course and when darkness fell, continued by the light of acetylene lamps carried by four helpful caddies.

He played right through the night and on and on the next day until finally, at

BRAM STOKER

Pedestrian and creator of *Dracula*

7.30 p.m. and after almost 36 hours of continuous golf, he could go no further. He had completed 14 full rounds at an absurd average of one every 2½ hours and hit well over 1,000 shots. It was, however, all too much for him. His appetite for playing the game was unfortunately far greater than his constitution could bear and he never recovered from his efforts. He died a few years later, a broken man.

Richard Sutton This sporting gentleman invented, played and still holds the record for the Streets of London Golf Course. These alfresco links, stretching from E1 to SW1, came temporarily into being in 1939 when Sutton accepted a bet that he could not play his way from Tower Bridge to White's Club in St James's Street in under 200 strokes.

Taking the precaution of starting in the early hours of the morning to avoid traffic and pedestrians, he teed off from the Bridge and began golfing his way across the metropolis. He used a putter and despite nearly holing out down a couple of drains, he eventually managed to roll the ball up to the doorway of his club to finish the 6,500 yard course in 142 strokes and win the wager easily.

Fred Swindell The most aptly named bookmaker who ever lived. Although he had the most off-putting name in the business this former Derby labourer had so many people place bets with him that he was able to retire a wealthy man. The reason, perhaps, was that Mr Swindell was said to be totally honest and nineteenth century punters trusted him implicitly with their investments. A curious part of his integrity was a refusal to countenance bets on anything other than horse racing. He particularly disapproved of gambling on athletics matches and once warned Sir John Astley, 'Never back anything as can talk.'

T

Mr Tarbet An impressively zealous football referee, he not only booked all 11 players and both substitutes of Glencraig United but did so in the dressing room before the match had ever begun. Not a ball, let alone a player, had yet been kicked in anger.

The incident happened on 2 February 1975. As Mr Tarbet arrived at the ground near Clydebank in Scotland he could hear the distinct sounds of chanting coming from the United dressing room. When he got closer he realised that the subject of the rhyme was himself, or rather certain aspects of himself. This, he must have thought, is a flagrant breach of the Rules of the Game, section 12, sub-section m (ungentlemanly conduct) and he was not going to stand for it. He booked all 13 members of the chorus and then went out and supervised a somewhat anti-climactic 2-2 draw.

Stella Taylor Former Catholic nun who developed a passion for long-distance swimming. She broke records for the English Channel, Loch Ness and the straits between the Bahamas and Florida but her greatest performance was in a stretch of water no more than 55 yards across. This was the pool at the International Swimming Hall of Fame, Fort Lauderdale, Miami. She entered the water at 10 p.m. one Tuesday night in April 1982 and didn't emerge until three o'clock on the Friday afternoon.

The 52-year-old Stella spent the intervening 65 hours swimming up and down the pool 3,120 times, covering an estimated 175 miles and comfortably demolishing her existing record. She had kept herself going on a diet of honey, rice, egg salad and cheese but in spite of this when she climbed out she appeared to have shrunk a bit. However, pool manager Joe Schoren was reassuring, 'Her skin was a little shrivelled,' he commented, 'but no more than you would expect after spending nearly three days in the water.'

Lionel, Lord Tennyson (1889–1951) When it came to taking a sporting chance Lionel Tennyson, grandson of the poet, cricket captain of Hampshire and England and late of the Rifle Brigade, was never found wanting. Whether it was playing one of the most daring innings in Test cricket, breaking bones in steeplechases, being banned from a country house for his behaviour at the billiard table, annoying the MCC or gambling away more in a week than some men earned in a lifetime, he never once flinched from taking a risk.

His daredevil temperament first emerged during a visit he paid as a boy to Taplow Court, the Thameside home of Lord Desborough. Winston Churchill was also a caller and the young Tennyson and his pals watched the great man as he stood in his frock coat and top hat talking to Lady Desborough on the riverbank. As Tennyson later wrote, 'The sight of him orating and gesticulating in those clothes so near the water was too great a temptation for us to resist.' The lads charged from behind, sending the future Prime Minister tumbling into the Thames with a satisfyingly large splash. Only the intercession of a drenched but sporting Churchill saved Tennyson from a terrible beating.

Between pranks he played some promising cricket and by the time he entered the army in 1909 he had a ready-made reputation for brash, attacking batsmanship. The regiment he joined was the Coldstream Guards, then, if the officer chose it, little more than a glorified excuse to pursue sport full time. Tennyson wasted no opportunity. Not only was there cricket but horse racing, where you could lose large sums of money, and steeplechasing with its ample scope for breaking bones. He also threw himself into hunting, golf, football, shooting, billiards and hockey.

In some of these activities there was the chance both to lose money and injure himself, as in the 1911 Coldstream Plate where he fell at the last, snapped his collar-bone and ruined a good bet. Even dodgier escapades followed, like the time he invited half a dozen Gaiety Girls to enliven a cold Christmas night's guard duty at the Tower of London and was caught, red-handed so to speak. Then there was the smashing of a vast, priceless mirror at Broke Hall in Suffolk while playing an illicit game of billiard fives (a lethal sport which involves one player trying to hit the balls into the pockets as hard as he can while his opponent attempts to catch or deflect them). Sure enough, as the mad contest intensified, Tennyson hit a shot which rose from the table like a Guy Fawkes

LIONEL, LORD TENNYSON

Attacking batsman and reckless gambler

rocket and shattered the mirror into a million fragments. He left shame-faced at first light, failed ever to compose a note of apology and, not surprisingly, was never invited to the hall again.

Even if he did not have to pay for this piece of damage his lifestyle still imposed severe burdens on his income and, ever the risk-taker, he tried to swell his coffers by betting. At first, when he confined his investments mainly to Alexandra Park racecourse, he seemed unable to lose. But then, in one spectacular week just before the Great War, he managed to convert a bank balance of £5,000 into the most catastrophic of debts.

It all started at Hurst Park where he lost £1,000 in one afternoon. That was the good day. After that it was downhill all the way and the next two days at Newbury cost him over £4,000. Now in debt and gambling on credit, he went straight to the meeting at Windsor in a frantic bid to recoup his losses. Instead he lost more than he had done in the other days' racing put together. In a little over a week he had lost £12,000 and was now £7,000 in debt.

There was nothing for it but to go home, confess all and face the unpleasant music. It was the predictable scene – mother in tears, father outraged and plenty of hand-wringing on behalf of the culprit – but the upshot was that the debts were paid and Tennyson was transferred to the Rifle Brigade. It seemed an odd choice, for he was no marksman and in later life brought a panther shoot to a halt by gunning down the tethered goat that was being used as bait. But the Brigade was cheaper than the Guards and offered fewer temptations, and it was with them that he was wounded three times in the ensuing war.

Shortly after the return of peace, Tennyson resigned from the Army and settled down to concentrate on cricket. As captain of Hampshire he was a complete law unto himself. He used to send messages out from the pavilion to his men while they were batting and when the umpires objected to this he sent a telegram instead. He was also the first county skipper to lead his professionals out of the hallowed amateurs-only centre gate at Lord's and cared not a damn when the MCC president took him to task. Indeed it was said that his men would follow him anywhere and in the case of the wicket-keeper Walter Livesey this was quite literally so, for he was also Tennyson's personal servant.

When he came to captain England for the first time, in the Third Test against Australia in 1921, he led by magnificent example, scoring one of the most remarkable innings of all time. The scene was set during Australia's first innings when Tennyson injured his hand so badly that it needed three stitches and was, to all intents and purposes, rendered useless. It was the last thing his side needed. Australia had made 407 and with Hobbs in hospital England were soon in desperate trouble at 67 for 5. Johnny Douglas played a good innings but when the eighth wicket fell, safety was still a long way off.

It was then that Tennyson decided to chance his one good arm against the feared pace of Macdonald and Gregory. To the amazement of everyone in the ground he emerged from the pavilion, strode to the wicket and began setting about the attack one-handed. Using his bat like a tennis racket he was a wonder to behold and scored 63 in a little over an hour. He had not only saved the follow-on but hit ten fours into the bargain. When the sides batted again he rounded off his heroic performance by taking a catch and scoring 36 more one-armed runs, including a six. It was the kind of florid finishing touch such as his grandfather would have added to one of his poems. But then Lionel, the third Lord Tennyson, always did save his most inspired moments for his sport.

Dr Sherman A. Thomas If there was one thing that drove this American golfer mad it was the sound of any interruption while he putted. Absolute silence was required and his partners had always respected this. So when in 1982 he hunched over a putt on the 17th green of the Congressional Country Club, Washington D.C., his obliging comrades stood rigidly to attention, assumed an unblinking stare and held their breath. All was therefore tranquillity as Dr Thomas drew back his putter to make his careful stroke.

Then, at the critical moment, there came from off the green the sudden and unmistakable honk of a Canada goose. The effect was immediate and profound. Thomas reacted as if receiving a substantial electric shock and in his nervous spasm could only jab the ball wide of the hole. He swirled round to confront the culprit, who was by now padding quietly away from the scene with as innocent an air as it could manage. Shaking with rage he rode after the bird, took deliberate aim and pole-axed it with a devastating putt to the head.

The poor goose may have been dead but it had its revenge. Geese were out of season and several weeks later Dr Thomas appeared in court on the appropriate charge and he was fined $500.

Major Towse VC A war hero and pioneer golfer. He lost his sight during the South African War in 1899 but did not think this was any reason to put his feet up. Not only did he carry on with his rowing but he also decided to take up golf – the first blind man ever to do so.

As befits a holder of the Victoria Cross, he was determined not to be given special treatment and would only allow two minor concessions to his disablement. The first was that he should be permitted to touch the ball with his hands to tell its position and the second was that his caddie could ring a small bell to indicate the direction of the hole. In this fashion he enjoyed nearly 40 years of sightless golf.

G. M. Trevelyan Alone among historians this distinguished scholar correctly diagnosed one of the prime causes of the French Revolution – the lack of cricket in that unhappy land. Writing in his magnum opus *English Social History*, he observed, 'If the French noblesse had been capable of playing cricket with their peasants, their chateaux would never have been burnt.' The Russian aristocracy were similarly stubborn and sure enough, 128 years later, they paid the penalty.

Albert Trott (1873–1914) The cricketer who ruined his own benefit match. It happened at Lord's in 1907 when the all-rounder, who had played in Tests for both Australia and England, found the temptations of Somerset's soft middle order too great to resist. He took four wickets in five balls and then polished off the tail with a hat-trick – thus severely curtailing the game and robbing himself of large amounts of much-needed gate money. As the final Somerset wicket fell he wailed, 'I've bowled myself into the workhouse.'

The situation was not quite as bad as that but it was a close call. After a couple more desultory seasons his health began to fail and he turned to umpiring. In time Trott found even that a struggle. He was not strong and, lacking the means to seek a better climate, his condition worsened considerably. One day in 1914 he arranged his modest effects at his lodgings in Willesden Green and shot himself through the head. The man whose enthusiasm at his benefit match had cost him a small fortune left his wardrobe to his landlady and just £4 in cash.

Major Philip Trevor A military man of unsophisticated views who obviously divided the world into cricketers and unacceptable specimens called foreigners. Towards the end of the nineteenth century he wrote, 'When you find a man completely out of sympathy with cricket you will generally find some other rather un-English trait in his character.'

V

Gaston Vareilles French rugby player whose international career consisted of half a train journey. He was selected to play at centre for France against Scotland in 1911. On his way to the match he began to feel hungry, so when the train stopped at a junction he nipped off to buy a sandwich. Unfortunately he failed to get back on time, was left behind, missed the game and was never chosen to represent his country again.

Venturers Cricket Club A bunch of determined fanatics based in trouble-torn Aden who continued to play up and play the game despite the civil war that raged around them. Even if the shelling from Yemeni nationalists threatened to pick off the fieldsmen one by one, these phlegmatic characters in white would never consider an abandonment, only the briefest of temporary interruptions. Their splendid attitude was typified by this immortal line from their scorebook for August 1967, 'Play delayed ten minutes by mortar attack.'

Bill Veeck The manager of the ailing St Louis Browns baseball team, his efforts to boost flagging attendances were so outrageous that they eventually got him banned from the game for life.

It was in 1951, after years of disastrous results, that he finally despaired of having a winning team to lure in the fans and so turned to more desperate measures. At first he tried bribery, buying 6,000 baseball bats from a bankrupt manufacturer and giving them away to the crowd. It seemed to work and spectators were soon being offered orchids from Hawaii, stepladders, cup cakes and even a limited number of live lobsters.

When the drawing power of free gifts wore off, Veeck went for something a little less conventional – an exploding scoreboard. The idea was that fireworks would erupt from it to the tune of Handel's 'Messiah' every time the Browns scored, which sadly was not that often.

A more reliable novelty were the midgets he employed to sell special midget hot-dogs. Indeed he was so taken with the appeal of very small human beings that he even signed one up to play in the team and when the Browns trotted out against Detroit Tigers there among them was 3 foot 7 inch Eddie Gaedel. Kitted out in a shirt appropriately numbered '⅛', the little crowd-puller went out to bat only once. He faced four pitches, failed to connect with any of them and was soon walking back to the team bench where his colleagues helped him clamber aboard.

It was not a happy episode. The punters were unimpressed, midgets were banned by the major leagues, Veeck was banned for life and after the team lost 20 consecutive home games in 1953, the franchise was transferred to Baltimore. Here normality reigned. The Orioles, as they became known, installed an ordinary scoreboard, served full-sized hot-dogs and hired players of at least average height. The fans, of course, flocked in and within a dozen years the team had won the World Series.

Nicholas Vladivar This Canadian athlete was in such dire need of sponsorship that he was prepared to do anything in return for some backing, even change his name. So when a firm of vodka manufacturers in Warrington stepped forward with some cash for him in 1980, Nicholas Akers took out a deed poll and became Nicholas Vladivar.

He ran under this name at the Commonwealth Games of 1982 but, judging by his slow performance, he should have been called Johnnie Walker instead. As a result Vladivar cancelled his contract and Nicholas was left with a silly and unprofitable surname. He immediately set about finding a new identity. 'Look,' he announced, 'I'm anyone's if the price is right. I'm quite prepared to become Nicholas Colgate, Nicholas Rice Krispies, Nicholas Newcastle Brown or Nicholas Aspirin as long as someone comes up with the cash to keep me running.'

W

Al Wacquie American mountaineer and the world champion at vertical running. On 1 March 1984 he ran up the stairs of the Empire State Building in New York, covering all 1,575 steps and 82 floors in 11 minutes 29 seconds.

Norman Waternorth A dogged little fellow who saw no reason why the loss of a leg should prevent him acting as captain and secretary of Gisburn Cricket Club in the 1930s. By the time that he finally hung up his pad, he had taken more than 1,000 wickets and scored 3,600 runs in 22 seasons of one legged cricket.

Jack Wattam The world's oldest footballer. This Grimsby enthusiast had started playing the game as a schoolboy in the early 1920s and he was still turning out in the local Sunday league 60-odd years later, at the age of 74. In between he had appeared in over 5,000 matches, a total which included playing twice a week right up until he was 69 years of age. This probably made him the only man ever to queue up for his pension with his football gear under his arm.

For the last 20 years of this marathon career, during which he was never booked or sent off, Wattam played for Weelsby Rovers. When he joined them they were in the first division of the local Sunday league but by 1982 they were bottom of the tenth with a forward line whose average age was 50. That season they lost all their 24 games, conceded 234 goals and scored a mere 25. But Wattam did not mind, as long as he was playing football he was happy. In December 1983 the 74-year-old even played on Weelsby's right wing just a few days before he went into hospital for a colostomy. It was dedication such as this that won him the Observer Sports Nut of the Year award in 1983.

G. J. V. Weighall A Cambridge University and Kent cricketer, he believed that the game transcended all other issues in life. When the great Frank Woolley was omitted from the England team he described it as, 'the greatest crime since the Crucifixion.'

Glenn Welt This computer programmer from Florida thought that there was only one way to support his beloved gridiron football team – and that was as a cheerleader. So he applied to join the Miami Dolphins' high-kicking, micro-skirted, pom-pom-waving chorus line. He said, 'I want to be part of the American tradition of leggy lovelies who bounce and chant to spur their team on.'

Not surprisingly they turned him down and when Mr Welt heard this he promptly filed a sex descrimination suit against the Dolphins' cheerleader group. 'Why deny a person the right to wear pantyhose, leotards and bobbles, to wave his shako and twiddle his stick?' he protested, 'I am an accomplished dancer and the Dolphins need a man to stimulate the lady fans.'

The club's defence to his action was devastatingly simple. 'There is one thing wrong with Mr Welt,' said Miss Maytree Lumble, the Dolphins' choreo-grapher, 'he is an ugly man.'

Revd Frederick Brooke Westcott A sporting zealot. As headmaster of Sher-borne School from 1888 to 1906 he raised the worship of games to new heights of fanaticism. Whatever the weather, every home match that the school played was accompanied by the spectacle of this strange figure, dressed in his cycling gear and a rat catcher's hat, running up and down the touchline in a partisan frenzy, screaming encouragement in English, Latin and Greek. He expected the same excessive level of commitment from his teams. If a boy could speak at the end of a match, the Revd Westcott took it as a sign that the youth had not given his all and he would soundly beat him.

When the school were playing away he would spend the afternoon in his study, fretting over the outcome. If the news was bad he would be thrown into such a depression that only a subsequent victory could lift it. News of a triumph, however, would send him into convulsions of pleasure. The local railwaymen would be instructed to put fog signals on the line to give the victors a rousing welcome and Revd Westcott would then preach a congratulatory sermon from the pulpit.

The old maniac also organised football matches with the few girls' schools that were rash enough to accept the challenge. He would join in these bizarre encounters but spent most of his time yelling, 'Run, woman, run,' at the female contestants and urging on the more reluctant sportswomen by swiping them with his stick.

White's Club During the eighteenth century the members of this London club were gamblers of the most rabid kind. Their motto seemed to be: if it moves, back it; if it doesn't, do it each way. But while horse racing, the turn of a card or throw of a dice were satisfactory up to a point, the well-heeled punters at White's were always on the look-out for less conventional ways of losing their money. So it was that anything which might happen in their public or private lives became fair game for a wager. The duration of wars, the marriage prospects of sisters and daughters, the health of their nearest and dearest – anything whose outcome was in the slightest doubt was liable to have large amounts of guineas riding on it.

Of course, had one Edward Danvers known of their appetite for such tasteless transactions he would probably have chosen the doorway of some other club in which to collapse. But, as is so often the case, this unfortunate Londoner had little choice about when and where he would slump unconscious to the ground. White's it was and it was into the discreetly stylish interior of the club that some well-meaning souls carried him.

Now had he remained on the pavement, all might yet have been well. But, according to novelist and man about town Horace Walpole, once inside the club, Danvers' uncertain condition – flickering between life and death – aroused the jaded interest of the drone-like members and soon an animated debate was in progress. Some thought he looked distinctly peaky and was unlikely to last the hour, others said this was rubbish and insisted that his drained pallor meant that he had fought off the crisis and would be up and about in no time. The pessimists invited the optimists to put their money where their medical opinions were and in an instant dozens of bets were being struck at various odds on whether poor Danvers would live or die.

The members were, however, agreed on one thing: it would be most irregular for the patient to be treated, since this would constitute 'interference with the wager'. So no physician was called and the sportsmen sat back and waited for nature to run its course. This it duly did, Danvers pegged out to give the pessimists a result and they merrily collected their winnings. (Some authorities have cast doubt on this story but it is included here because, apocryphal or not, it certainly reflects the desperate addiction to gambling among White's members at this time.)

Yorky Whiting Few men love their favourite football team as much as this

Devon dustman. He was so besotted with Fulham that he was prepared to travel 340 miles for each home game, paint his house in the team's colours and draw up a will leaving everything he owned to the club. This even included his house, called, quite naturally 'Craven Cottage' in honour of Fulham's ground.

This ludicrous dwelling was situated in the village of Topsham. Not only did it have black and white paintwork but the front hall was covered almost completely with Fulham programmes, hundreds more of which were stashed away in nearby cupboards. The barriers guarding the entrance to his garage were shaped like a set of goalposts and the entire effect was set off by the porch whose centrepiece was a carriage lamp bearing the features of Johnny Haynes, the club's most famous player.

Not content with these outward and visible signs of his devotion, the 59-year-old Yorky announced in 1966 that he would bequeath all his worldly wealth to Fulham. It was, he felt, the least he could do. Meanwhile, until they inherited, he would continue to support them in his own lavish way. 'I usually drop a pound or two in the kitty after a game,' he said, 'but if they needed it I'd gladly write them a cheque for £500.'

Lord George Wigg A politician and football supporter. His heady success at flushing the Profumo affair into the open must have played havoc with his sense of proportion, for when Poland knocked England out of the World Cup in 1973 he said, 'It's worse than losing a war, a national crisis of the highest magnitude.'

Bob Wilson and Michael Jones These two were so potty about football that in the course of a single season they watched a match at every League ground in the country. Just for good measure they even visited Berwick, who actually play in the Scottish competition. Their marathon started on 10 August 1968 and by the time they had finished, 264 days later, they had seen an average of nearly three games a week and sat through 8,370 minutes of football.

Christy Williams One of the biggest gluttons for punishment in ring history. It was, appropriately enough, on Boxing Day 1902 that this American lightweight came face to face with Oscar 'Battling' Nelson. But within minutes of climbing between the ropes at Hot Springs, Arkansas, Williams was wishing he was somewhere else. For every time he peeped out from behind his gloves, there was Nelson's fist homing in on his jaw. The next thing he knew he would be down on the deck looking up at the referee.

Most boxers would have got fed up after this happened for a tenth time, a few might even have survived 20 repeat performances but Williams was made of sterner stuff. He was knocked down no fewer than 41 times but on each occasion he came back for more. Finally, after going up and down like a yo-yo for 17 rounds, he dropped to the canvas for the 42nd time and wisely decided to stay there.

Plennie L. Wingo This American walking enthusiast was about as sensible as his name. Setting out on 15 April 1931 he walked the 8,000 miles from Santa Monica, California to Istanbul, Turkey, reaching his destination eighteen months later on 24 October 1932. He might have got there sooner if he had not walked the entire distance backwards.

Gary Winram Australian swimmer who was convinced that he would do better in the 1956 national championships if he was literally out of his mind. So just before he entered the water he had himself hypnotised to believe that he was being chased by a shark. He came second.

George Wilson A great early pedestrian and one of the few men ever to set a sporting record while in prison. Born in 1775, he had discovered his capacity for walking absurd distances while working as a tax collector, a job which often required him to cover up to 60 miles a week on foot. But before he had time to build much of a reputation as an athlete he was thrown into jail for debts and his walking days seemed over. Far from it. Freed from the distractions of collecting taxes, he was able to concentrate solely on his training, albeit in a confined space, and soon he had become the fastest man in captivity.

His first major challenge in the Fleet Prison was to walk round and round a yard measuring only 33 foot long by 25 foot across for 12 hours non-stop. When he finally came to a halt he had travelled 50 miles. Later he was able to extend his performance in this small arena to the dizzy lengths of 109 miles in 24 hours.

When Wilson was released from jail he launched himself on a new career, walking long distances for bets and by 1815 he was ready to attempt his most ambitious project yet – 1,000 miles in 500 hours. His plan was to cover 50 miles a day for 20 days by walking up and down between the Hare and Billet, Black-heath and a point half a mile up the road. So at 5.30 a.m. on Monday 11 September the 40-year-old Wilson set off.

For a time all was well. Each day he would cover the stipulated distance and after that was done he would be carried back to his sleeping quarters in a sedan chair and his feet would be bathed in salt water. Gradually, however, trouble began to loom. The problem was that Wilson was too successful. Word of his astonishing record attempt spread and the crowds drawn to Blackheath grew larger and larger. A fair rolled up and pitched their tents and soon every sensation-seeker, ne'er-do-well and pickpocket in London had arrived on the scene.

Despite the fuss Wilson kept on walking. But as his attempt entered the third week it all became too much for the local justices of the peace. Fearing that the crowd was liable to become a raging mob at the drop of a bad word from one of the assembled hooligans, the magistrates acted. On the morning of Tuesday 26 September the multitude began to disperse after the main attraction had failed to show up. Not of course that he had developed foot sores or retired. He could not come because the forces of law and order had placed him under house arrest.

Wilson was furious. At the time of his detention he had been only five days and less than 250 miles from his target. Now it was all over. The awful irony could not have escaped the old gaolbird – when it came to breaking walking records he had really been far better off in prison. At least he didn't get arrested there.

Jabez Wolfe One of the most indomitable characters in swimming history. Between 1906 and his death in 1943 he made no fewer than 22 attempts to swim the English Channel and not one of them was successful. Year after year he would go down to the beach at Dover, wade into the surf and splash out towards the Continent. Sure enough, time after time, his weak and near-lifeless form would be plucked defeated from the water, with France still a shallow haze on the horizon.

It did not matter what he did – swimming fast or slow, on his front or on his back, from England to France or France to England – the result was always the same. Once he did actually get to within a few hundred yards of the French coast but he was beaten by the tides. Even then he refused to concede that the Channel had got the better of him and he went to his grave insisting that this failure was due to him being washed back out to sea by the opening of the dock gates at Calais.

Ken Wood A football fan who was so affected by his favourite team's relegation to the Third Division in 1970 that he announced his intention to emigrate. It was the first time that Sheffield Wednesday had ever sunk so low and the painful prospect of his side playing the likes of Southend and Halifax was too much for Mr Wood to bear. 'I've torn up my rosette in disgust, burnt my scarf and given my rattle away.' He said, 'there's nothing to keep me here.' He was getting out just in time, for the next season Wednesday only missed dropping into the Fourth Division by a single point.

Y

Yabba (1878–1942) An outlandish Australian cricket spectator. For more than 30 years he was the ringleader of the notorious Hill at Sydney Cricket Ground. This was the section of the stadium where barracking became an art-form. Throughout a day's play the Hill's beery voices kept up a constant barrage of rough-house comments, much to discomfort of visiting batsmen, especially English ones. Yabba was the captain of this crowd and in time he was raised by his fellows to the status of a cult figure.

His real name was Stephen Harold Gascoigne and he earnt his living selling rabbits from a cart which he trundled round the South Sydney and Balmain suburbs. But when an important game came to the SCG, the cart would be put away and Yabba would stride off to the ground dressed in his white hawker's coat and carrying a hamper and a day's supply of beer. Once inside, he would take up his favoured position on the Hill and there, stripped to his braces in the heat, he would hold court. He was a magnificent sight, 14 stone of quivering chauvinism, booming out his raucous comments in a voice that carried to the far corners of the ground. He was indeed a national stereotype brought to life. With his legendary beer drinking, uncouth appearance and loud-mouthed behaviour, Yabba represented to many of his countrymen the very flower of Australian manhood.

Ron Yeomans This cricket devotee so admired the turf at first class grounds up and down the country that he started bringing bits home with him. By the late 1950s he had collected enough pieces to construct an entire lawn in his back garden and eventually the patchwork greensward contained samples from over 20 grounds, including all Test match venues.

Naturally everything was completely above board. As one would expect from a man who was the Hon. Secretary of the Northern Cricket Society and Chairman of the Council of Cricket Societies, he would not cut a single sod unless permission had first been obtained from the groundsman or some other club official. But once approval had been given for his strange project, Mr Yeomans would set to work. He would remove a piece of turf two feet square, secure it safely in a hessian sack and proudly carry it home on the train. Then, with due ceremony, it would be carefully laid into its allotted place.

The progress of each new piece of grass was lovingly monitored and to aid this task he drew up a map giving the location and origin of every turf on the lawn. The results often surprised him and in a letter to *The Times* in 1972 Mr Yeomans informed the spellbound readers that Fenner's, the Cambridge University ground, produced the most luxuriant growth while the Oval, scene of many a Test match, was 'very thin and crumbled'.

Dimitriou Yordanidis A Greek athlete. On 10 October 1976 he took 7 hours 33 minutes to complete a marathon. The Athens crowds were astonished; not by his slow speed but by the fact that he was able to finish the race in any time, for Yordanidis was 98 years old.

Z

Abd-El Kader Zaag North African cyclist whose hopes in the 1950 Tour de France were rudely extinguished by a rather decent bottle of house red. The problem for him in that year's race was the insufferable heat. During the Perpignan to Nimes stage it was especially oppressive and although Zaag struggled along for a while there came a point when he could take it no longer.

Now the French are more than happy to see foreigners suffer from most things but dehydration is not one of them and a friendly spectator was soon offering the cyclist a bottle of wine. Little realising the potency of the claret brewed hereabouts, Zaag emptied every last drop down his parched throat and after gesticulating his thanks, remounted and went on his way. He had not gone very far when he began to appreciate why the French treat the wines of this region with particular respect. For just a mile or so down the road, his brain cells, unused to the sudden infusion of countless milligrams of high-grade alcohol, began to go on the blink. The next thing he knew he had fallen from his bike.

For some minutes he sat dazed by the roadside, wondering who he was, where he was and what he was doing there. Then the penny dropped. He was a cyclist, this was the Tour de France and, yes, there was his bike. He sat on the saddle, took careful hold of the handlebars, gingerly put his feet on the pedals, pressed forward and cycled off – in the wrong direction. He was last seen pedalling furiously back towards Perpignan.

Babe Zaharias (1914–1956) The most extraordinary all-round sportswoman who ever lived. In between setting a world athletics record at the age of 16 and

BABE ZAHARIAS

The greatest sportswoman who ever lived

her cruelly premature death, she dedicated herself to coming first at whatever she did. And she did a scarcely credible number of things. She single-handedly beat every track and field club in America to win the 1932 national championships, captured two Olympic gold medals, won major golf championships on both sides of the Atlantic, was an All-American basketball player and excelled at diving, lacrosse, baseball and billiards.

Yet although she was supremely gifted, these triumphs were hard-earned. She was never rich, tangled repeatedly with officialdom, was banned by several sports and mastered golf only by practising until her hands bled. But her intense competitive spirit was always equal to the occasion and it is typical that she should give two of her greatest performances shortly after undergoing a major operation for cancer.

The Babe, as she was always known, was born to Norwegian parents as Mildred Didrikson in Port Arthus, Texas in 1914. Although she was an outstanding youngster at baseball and basketball, it was soon obvious that she had a rare talent for athletics. She broke the world javelin record while only 16 and two years later she accomplished one of the most outrageous day's work in track and field history.

The occasion was the national club championships in Chicago. As her club's sole representative the young prodigy was entered for seven events and for two and a half hours she dashed madly from place to place, pausing only to compete before rushing off to the next discipline. First it would be a heat in the 80 metres hurdles, then over to the high jump, followed by a quick throw of the javelin or shot, before she had to return to the track to run again. It was a schedule that would have worried a god, but the Babe lapped it up and by the end of the afternoon her hyperactivity had brought her astonishing success. Of seven events she entered, she came first in five, tied for the sixth and finished third in the last. She had won the club championship all on her own with 30 points, eight clear of her nearest rivals who needed no fewer than 22 athletes to reach even that total.

A few months later came the Los Angeles Olympics. Had there not been a rule limiting women to three events, the 18-year-old Zaharias would probably have gone through the card. But as it was she had to be content with coming first in the javelin, hurdles and high jump and only a debatable technicality in the latter event robbed her of three gold medals.

Yet by that December her track and field career was over. Attempting to make some much-needed cash out of her Olympic victories, America's new teenage heroine had endorsed a sales campaign for a car. The authorities were horrified and they banned her from amateur athletics for life. For a while she played baseball and basketball professionally and toured in a vaudeville act performing acrobatics and playing the mouth organ. But although she made quite a name for herself at baseball – once hitting three home runs in a game – none of these activities satisfied her appetite for real competitive sport. So in 1934 she settled down and began to apply every ounce of herself to learning golf.

Her regime was dedication run riot. At weekends she practised 12–16 hours a day, while during the week she was up at the crack of dawn hitting balls from 5.30 to 8.30 before going to the office. Lunchtime was a quick sandwich followed by practice in the boss's office, putting on the carpet and chipping balls into a leather chair. She left work at 3.30 p.m., had an hour's lesson and then hit golf balls until dark. She wrote later, 'I'd hit balls until my hands were bloody and sore. I'd have tape all over my hands and blood all over the tape.' Then it was home to dinner and an early retirement with a golf book to study.

In just over a year this punishing routine paid off and she won the Texas Amateur. But before she could prove herself further, the golf authorities banned her from amateur tournaments for having played other sports professionally. (Tennis officials were to take the same action when she flirted briefly with that game.) So for a time she had to be content with playing exhibition golf tournaments. But then in 1938 came the event that was to lead her back to amateur sport: she got married.

Her husband was a 20 stone wrestler called George Zaharias and fighting under the name of 'The Crying Greek from Cripple Creek' he earned enough for the Babe to apply for reinstatement as an amateur golfer. She practised relentlessly and proved herself by refusing the prize money when she won professional events like the 1940 Western and Texas Opens. By 1943 she was re-admitted to the unpaid ranks and when she got down to serious tournament play after the war the world of women's golf hardly knew what hit it.

She won the US Amateur Championship in 1946 and, in the course of that year and the next, won 17 consecutive events including the 1947 British Amateur. Having made her point, she then turned professional and began dominating that scene with a game that was remarkable for long hitting. No lesser contemporary than Byron Nelson, twice US Masters champion, said that she could out-drive all but six men professionals.

Zaharias won the US Open in 1948, repeated the feat in 1950 when she won six out of the nine events on the tour and in 1951 came first in half the events she played. Two more victories followed in 1952 but by then her health was failing. Cancer was diagnosed and in 1953 she underwent major surgery. Against all advice she was back playing golf within a few weeks and just three and a half months after the operation she finished third in the US Open.

A year later she won the US Open Championship by the record margin of 12 strokes. It was to be her farewell performance in the event, for the cancer had returned and another operation in 1955 prevented her defending her title. The following year she was too ill for golf. Babe Zaharias had finally run up against an opponent even she could not beat and within a few months she was dead, aged just 42.

Matthias Zdarsky (1874–1946) This Alpine enthusiast was so addicted to skiing that he refused to give up the sport, even after suffering the most appalling injuries imaginable. While serving as a ski instructor with the Austrian Army during the First World War, he was trapped in an avalanche and sustained no fewer than 80 fractures and dislocations, including six separate ones in his spine. Walking, never mind skiing, seemed out of the question. But Zdarsky was determined to get back on the slopes. After studying the problem long and hard, he designed a special apparatus to support his near lifeless limbs and, to the wonderment of all but himself, he was able to ski again.

Charles Zibelman (b. 1894) One of the strangest swimmers ever to attempt a crossing of the English Channel. This American came over in 1933 with the intention of not only swimming from England to France but declaring that he would also smoke 50 cigars on the way. The boast was, of course, tempting the Channel fates a little too much and sure enough, after 12 hours, he was badly stung on the lip by a jellyfish and had to retire.

Had that been all there was to Zibelman, his effort might have become merely an obscure postscript to the history of this intimidating challenge. But as a swimmer he had a far more genuine claim to attention than an extravagant taste for Havana tobacco, for Charles Zibelman had no legs.

His handicap may have given rise to his rather tasteless nickname of 'Zimmy the Human Fish' but it did not prevent him developing into the greatest endurance swimmer of all time. In 1932 he had warmed up for his Channel bid by remaining in the water in Hawaii for 100 hours. Nine years later he set a record which is unbroken to this day. Entering a pool in Honolulu on 17 February 1941, he stayed there swimming almost continuously for an entire calendar week.

Bahige Zuhairy An intrepid Lebanese surfer, he found in-shore activities a little tame and so decided to paddle his board all the way across the Mediterranean. He fixed himself up with an escort boat and on 18 September 1964 set out from St George's Bay, Beirut and began working his way towards Cyprus, 150 miles away.

All went well until the second evening when rough seas sprang up. Zuhairy, perched on top of his flimsy craft, weathered the storm; which is more than can be said for the boat accompanying him, the 42 foot cruiser Riana. Both engines were put out of action, she began to drift and her crew lost sight of the little figure on the surf board.

This was not quite how things were supposed to be. The men whose job it was to help Zuhairy find his way across the ocean now had to wait until they were found themselves, by the air-sea rescue team. Somewhat later than intended, the Riana made a rather undignified entrance into port at the end of a tugboat's tow-rope. Meanwhile Zuhairy, finding himself all alone, had simply got his head down and set off in what he hoped was the general direction of Cyprus. Fortunately he guessed right and, after ten miles of solitary paddling, he slid onto the beach at Greco Bay, Famagusta to complete his ludicrous journey in 38 hours 40 minutes.

Bibliography

Newspapers
The Times, Daily Telegraph, Guardian, Daily Express, Sunday Express, Daily Mail, Sun, Observer, Croydon Advertiser, South London Press.

Periodicals
Golf World, Golf Monthly, Sports Illustrated, Sport and Leisure, The Cricketer.

General Sport
The Game All volumes Marshal Cavendish.
Abrahams, Harold and Bruce-Kerreds, J. *Oxford v Cambridge* Faber 1931.
Arlott, John ed. *The Oxford Companion to Sports and Games* Oxford University Press 1976.
Arnold, Peter *The Encyclopaedia of Gambling* Collins 1978.
Brown, Craig and David *The Book of Sports Lists* Arthur Barker 1983.
Fuller, Peter *The Champions* Allen Lane 1978.
Harvey, Charles ed. *Encyclopaedia of Sports and Sportsmen* Sampson Low 1966.
Harvey, Charles ed. *Sports International* Sampson Low 1960.
Harvey, Charles ed. *Encyclopaedia of Sport* Sampson Low 1960.
Jewell, Brian *Sports and Games* Midas Books 1977.
Pannick, David *Sex Discrimination in Sport* Equal Opportunities Commission 1983.
Ray, Phillip ed. *Rothman's Atlas of World Sport* Rothmans Publications 1982.

Sports History
Brasch, R. *How Did Sports Begin?* Longman 1972.
Finlay, M. I. and Pleket, H. W. *The Olympic Games* Chatto and Windus 1976.
Mandell, Richard D. *Sport: A Cultural History* Columbia University Press 1984.
Olivova, Vera *Sport and Games in The Ancient World* Orbis 1984.
Strutt, Joseph *The Sports and Pastimes of the People of England* Methuen 1801.

Athletics
Gynn, Roger *The Guinness Book of the Marathon* Guinness Superlatives 1984
Lovesey, Peter *The Official Centenary History of the Amateur Athletics Association* Guinness Superlatives 1979.
Quercetani, Roberto Luigi *A World History of Track and Field Athletics 1864–1964* Oxford University Press 1964.

Boxing
Golesworthy, Maurice *The Encyclopaedia of Boxing* Robert Hale 1975.
Odd, Gilbert *The Encyclopaedia of Boxing* Hamlyn 1983.

Cricket
Altham, H. S. and Swanton, E. W. *A History of Cricket* George Allen and Unwin 1938.
Barty-King, Hugh *Quilt Winders and Pod Shavers. The History of Cricket Bat and Ball Manufacture* Macdonald and Janes 1979.
Brookes, Christopher *English Cricket* Weidenfeld and Nicholson 1979.
Frith, David *The Fast Men* Corgi revised edition 1977.
Gibson, Alan *The Cricket Captains of England* Cassell 1979.
Green, Benny ed. *Wisden Anthology 1864–1900* Queen Anne Press 1979.
Green, Benny ed. *Wisden Anthology 1940–1963* Queen Anne Press 1982.
Howat, Gerald *Village Cricket* David and Charles 1980.
Marshall, Howard ed. *Cricket Stories* Putnam 1933.
Martin-Jenkins, Christopher *The Complete Who's Who of Test Cricketers* Orbis 1980.
Mell, George *This Curious Game of Cricket* George Allen and Unwin 1982.
Pesket, Roy ed. *The Best of Cricket* Hamlyn 1982.
Pollard, Jack *Australian Cricket: The Game and the Players* Hodder and Stoughton 1982.
Simm, Robert and Smart, Alastair *The Art of Cricket* Secker and Warburg 1983.
Swanton, E. W. and Woodcock, John *Barclay's World of Cricket* Collins 1980.
Webber, Roy *The Book of Cricket Records* Phoenix 1961.

Williams, Marcus ed. *The Way to Lord's. Cricketing Letters to the Times* Collins/Willow 1983.
Wisden Cricketers' Almanac Various editions 1864–1984.

Football
Ball, Peter and Shaw, Phil *The Book of Football Quotations* Stanley Paul 1984.
Corrigan, Peter *100 years of Welsh Soccer* Welsh Brewers Ltd 1976.
Gibson, Alfred and Pickford, William *Association Football and the Men Who Made It* Caxton 1906.
Glanville, Brian ed. *The Footballer's Companion* Eyre and Spottiswoode 1962.
Golesworthy, Maurice *The Encyclopaedia of Association Football* Robert Hale 1976.
Inglis, Simon *The Football Grounds of England and Wales* Collins/Willow 1983.
Soar, Phil *The Hamlyn A–Z of British Football Records* Hamlyn 1981.
Walvin, James *The People's Game* Allen Lane 1975.

Golf
Allis, Peter *The Who's Who of Golf* Orbis 1983.
Cossey, Rosalynde *Golfing Ladies* Orbis 1984.
Dobereiner, Peter ed. *The Golfers* Collins 1982.
Huggins, Percy ed. *The Golfer's Handbook* The Golfers Handbook Ltd 1983.
Menzies, Gordon ed. *The World of Golf* BBC Publications 1982.
The Richmond Golf Club Official Handbook Richmond G.C.
Steel, Donald *The Guinness Book of Golf Facts and Feats* Guinness Superlatives 1980.
Tressider, Phil *The Golfer Who Laughed* Stanley Paul 1975.
Wilson, Mark and Bowden, Ken eds. *The Best of Henry Longhurst* 1979.

Horse Racing
Fawcett, William *Sporting Spectacle* Methuen 1939.
Francis, Dick and Welcome, John eds. *The Racing Man's Bedside Book* Faber 1963.
Longrigg, Roger *The History of Horse Racing* MacMillan 1972.

Swimming
Rockett, Sam *It's Cold in the Channel* Hutchinson 1956.
British Long Distance Swimming Association Handbook BLDSA 1982.

Tennis
Atkin, Ronald *The Book of Wimbledon* Heinemann 1981.
Robertson, Max *Wimbledon 1877–1977* Arthur Barker 1977.

Tingay, Lance *100 Years of Wimbledon* Guinness Superlatives 1977.
Todd, T *The Tennis Players* Vallancey 1979.

Other Sports
Dodd, Christopher *The Oxford and Cambridge Boat Race* Stanley Paul 1983.
Everton, Clive *The Guinness Book of Snooker* Guinness Superlatives 1981.

Olympic Games
Cook, Sir Theodore ed. *The Fourth Olympiad. The Official Report of the Olympic Games of 1908* British Olympic Association 1909.
Greenberg, Stan ed. *The Guinness Book of Olympic Facts and Feats* Guinness Superlatives 1983.
Guiney, David *The Dunlop Book of the Olympics* Eastland Press 1972.
Killanin, Lord and Rodda, John eds. *The Olympic Games* Macdonald and Janes 1979.
Various *The History of the Olympics* Marshall Cavendish 1980.
Wallechinsky, David *The Complete Book of the Olympics* Penguin Books 1984.

Biography
Dictionary of National Biography Oxford University Press.
Who's Who Adam and Charles Black.
Who Was Who Adam and Charles Black.
Who Did What Mitchell Beazley 1979.
Darwin, Bernard *W. G. Grace* Duckworth 1934.
Einberg, Elizabeth *Gainsborough's Giovanna Bacelli* Tate Gallery 1976.
Frith, David *My Dear Victorious Stod. A Biography of A. E. Stoddart* Lutterworth Press 1967.
Gerson, Noel B. *Lillie Langtry* Robert Hale.
Hardwick, Michael and Mollie *The Man Who Was Sherlock Holmes* John Murray 1964.
Longford, Elizabeth *Byron* Hutchinson 1976.
Midwinter, Eric *W. G. Grace* George Allen and Unwin 1981.
Mosley, Nicholas *Julian Grenfell. The Life and Times of His Death 1888–1915* Weidenfeld and Nicholson 1976.
Osbaldeston, George *Squire Osbaldeston: His Autobiography* John Lane and The Bodley Head 1926.
Plomer, William ed. *Kilvert's Diary* Penguin Books 1977.
Roberts, Brian *The Mad Bad Line* Hamish Hamilton 1981.

Sutherland, Douglas *The Yellow Earl. The Life of Hugh Lowther, 5th Earl of Lonsdale 1857–1944* Cassell 1965.
Symons, Julian *Conan Doyle. Portrait of An Artist* Andre Deutsch 1979.
Tennyson, Lionel Lord *From Verse To Worse* Cassell 1933.
Tennyson, Lionel Lord *Sticky Wickets* Christopher Johnson 1950.
Turner, E. S. *Amazing Grace* Michael Joseph 1975.
Wallace, Irving, Amy and Sylvia and Wallechinsky, David *The Intimate Sex Lives of Famous People* Hutchinson 1981.

Social History
Bamford, T. W. *The Rise of the Public Schools* Nelson 1967.
Barrow, Andrew *Gossip 1920–1970* Hamish Hamilton 1978.
Chesney, Kellow *The Victorian Underworld* Temple Smith 1970.
Collins, Brenda *Victorian Country Parsons* Constable 1977.
Kuznetsov, Anatoli *Babi Yar* Jonathan Cape 1970.
Longmate, Norman *How We Lived Then* Hutchinson 1971.
Longrigg, Roger *The English Squire and His Sport* Michael Joseph 1977.
Mason, Philip *The English Gentleman* André Deutsch 1982.
Trevelyan, G. M. *Illustrated English Social History. Volume 3 Pelican* 1966.
Turner, E. S. *Boys Will Be Boys* Michael Joseph 1948.

Curiosities
The Readers Digest Book of Strange Stories and Amazing Facts Readers Digest 1975.
Beadle, Jeremy *Today's the Day* W. H. Allen 1979.
Bowler, Peter and Green Jonathan *What A Way To Go* Pan 1983.
Caulfield, Catherine *The Emperor of the United States and Other Magnificent British Eccentrics* Routledge and Kegan Paul 1981.
Parsons, Denys *Funny Ho-Ho and Funny Fantastic* Pan 1967.
Sieveking, George ed. *Man Bites Man. The Scrapbook of an Edwardian Eccentric* Jay Landesman 1980.
Sitwell, Edith *English Eccentrics* Faber and Faber 1933.
Timbs, John *English Eccentrics and Eccentricities* Chatto 1897.
Wallechinsky, David and Wallace, Irving and Amy *The Book of Lists 1* Cassell 1977.
Wallechinsky, David and Wallace, Irving, Amy and Sylvia *The Book of Lists 2* Elm Tree 1980.
Wallechinsky, David and Wallace, Irving and Amy *The Book of Lists 3* Elm Tree 1983.

General Reference
Burke's Peerage Burke's Peerage Ltd 1963.
Asimov, Isaac *The Book of Facts* Hodder and Stoughton 1980.
Isaacs, Alan *The Macmillan Encyclopaedia* Macmillan 1981.
McWhirter, Norris *The Guinness Book of Records* Guinness Superlatives. Various editions 1965–1982.
Wood, Gerald *The Guinness Book of Animal Facts and Feats* Guinness Superlatives 1972.